SOCIAL MEDIA AND INDIAN YOUTH

SOCIAL MEDIA AND INDIAN YOUTH

Sanjay Singh Baghel

यात्रा
YATRA
BOOKS
An imprint of Vani Prakashan Group

Hardcover Firest Edition : 2025

vaniprakashan.com

YATRA BOOKS

VANI PRAKASHAN GROUP

Yatra Books is an imprint of Vani Prakashan Group

Head Office

4695, 21-A, Daryaganj, New Delhi-110 002, India
Phone : +91 11 23273167, 23275710

Registered Bookstores and Offices

Ashok Rajpath, Patna-800 004, Bihar
Coffee House Campus, Mahatma Gandhi Marg, Prayagraj-211 001, Uttar Pradesh
Mahatma Gandhi Antarrashtriya Hindi Vishwavidyalaya, Wardha-442 001, Maharashtra
sales@vaniprakashan.in
vaniprakashan@gmail.com

Social Media and Indian Youth

by Sanjay Singh Baghel

ISBN : 978-93-5775-580-1
Social Media

Price : ₹ 625

Printed and bound in India at City Press, Delhi-110095

Dedicated to my beloved parents

Late Smt. Mithilesh Kumari Singh

and

Late Shri Narendra Singh ji

Preface

Social networking sites (SNS's) have become imperative to the lives of youth today. They are a compulsive and addictive behaviour to our modern adolescence. Facebook, twitter, LinkedIn and other networking sites have not only given them a platform to interact, discuss and remain in touch with their loved ones who live at places across the globe but also to voice their opinions on social issues. It has created nothing less than a revolution across the world. The recent Jan Lokpal Bill Movement led by Anna Hazare and his team, and Nirbhaya Gang Rape case movement are uprising examples of SNS's where youths created mass awareness across the society. They not only participated to create a movement but also voiced their opinions through the various social networking sites mobilizing people to sign online petitions, sending them across to the respective authorities. It was an eye-opening example for any country and government to understand the power of social networking sites.

The SNS's have not only made a significant change in their personal and social lives, but also played a crucial role in breaking boundaries, crossing nations, and enabling them to communicate and share their view on issues like violation of human rights, girl's education, adverse effects of global warming, wrong deeds of political leaders, crime against women, corruption etc.

On one hand where social networking sites empower the youth and enable them to grow up to their social circle in term of their own acquaintances, on the other it raises many questions about their lifestyles, safety, privacy and legal issues. In this project we shall try to understand the impact of these networking sites on the lifestyles of Indian youths. Not only is that it a very subjective issue to make opinion about their thought, sociological and psychological change in their Behaviours too.

There is no doubt social media industry in India is run by young and educated youths in big cities and town. According to Analysis and Outlook social media in India 2012 in 2011 Indian SNS market saw a tremendous growth in the rise of the number of users and their participations, terms of time spent. While Telecom Regulatory Authority of India has written their report "there has been rapid rise in the number of internet users in India and has reached 21 million users in 2011. Broadband too has seen significant growth in 2011with13.30 million users (22%, Youth Organizations Umbrella, Inc. Y. O. U) compared to 10.92 million users in 2010 and was expected to reach 15.9 million users by end of 2012. 80% of the internet users are urban users and 20% are rural users in India and educated young people. Indians migrate to United States (US) for education and jobs and most of them will be in constant touch with friends in India which led to the rise in usage of social networks and it was even more increased as US companies set up offices in India employing thousands of people here, Indians using more technology products like mobiles, laptops, other computing devices like PCs, tablets and finally the voyeuristic appeal with open networks drove the usage further. Most popular social networking site in India is Facebook as recently it has dethroned Indonesia from the number 2 slot with 46 million monthly active users in February2012 on the site, an increase of 132% from the prior year. Urban cities like Mumbai, Delhi, Chennai, Kolkata, Bangalore, Hyderabad, Pune, Ahmedabad, and other tier 1and 2 cities and towns dominate the social networking usage in India. 75% is dominated by male and mostly the young students and professionals in the age group of 18-24 are dominating the social media usage followed by the 25-34 age group. They spend hours every month on the various social networking sites and actively engage with friends and others. Most of the users are using social media to stay in touch with friends, track and update their activities, social gaming, follow groups and communities, discuss social, political cultural and entertainment topics and also look for information about brands, products and also provide their feedback."

A research study was undertaken for the purpose of exploring the broad dimensions of the impact of social networking sites on the Indian youths, changing their mind sets and their lifestyles. Further it aims at exploring the potential possibilities for developing a knowledge-based society and enhancing their quality of life.

The book is of immense importance to the ones, who wants to understand social media and its importance on Indian youths. It will provide an insight to the students, educationists, researchers, media planners, social media users and policy makers. The authors trust that the book is an asset for all of us as we all are affected and attached in some means to the next generation revolution of social media.

— **Prof. Sanjay Singh Baghel**

Acknowledgements

From a simple discussion with my colleague and better half and the co-editor of the ready text, the book has gone through with its own journey. When we came to know about the innovation projects in our university, we decided to work together on an aspect which is of utmost importance and relevance not only to the current times but has an oceanic future in the times to come. Once we were able to give a shape to our idea we got the support from a fellow colleague, Ms. Geetanjali Batra from Commerce Department who agreed to become the co-investigator and further as required ten students across different departments were selected for the project.

Our idea from a bud to a loaded tree has taken shape in the form of this book. It has gone through unending long discussions, tea-time meetings, following and filling up questionnaires from Mumbai to Delhi and undoubtedly unstinted support of friends and family. We are indeed highly indebted to all our students who have been associated with this book and devoted their valuable time to bring an imagination into reality.

At the outset, being the editor of the book, I wish to thank all the respondents who have spared their valuable time and meticulously furnished data for numerous studies incorporated in the book. Without them this would have been remained but an idea and discussion. I would also like to thank our college students, young teachers at our college and other different institutions based in Delhi who very patiently agreed to furnish information and filled up our lengthy questionnaire. In Mumbai, I would like to thank my friend Mr. Shailendra Singh, Bank of Baroda who helped in collecting data for the same. I extend my humble gratitude to the institutions which served as the scope of the research studies and facilitated access to their institutions. A special thanks to the Heads of social media Cells of the three most prominent political parties of our country namely Mr. Vishesh Singh, AICC, Mr. Navrang, BJP and Mr. Ankit Lal, AAP. Without their support the special insights and realities could not have been presented. And above all, a special thanks to our project mentor Prof. Ashok Chakradhar, well known poet, writer, and techno-savvy Guru. His time, direction and focus gave us new possibilities to improvise our book.

We are also thankful and obliged to our college research team members Prof. Uma S. Singh and Dr. Geetanjali Batra (as Co-project Director), Associate Professor, Department of Management study, JNU, Delhi and our research students Vaishali Soni, Neha, Sumit Haldar, Akshay Saraswat, Yamini Nayar, Shreya Raheja, Kshitij Rai Handa , Himanshi Madan, Siddharth Rawal and Ashish Dwevedi, for their tireless and unconditional support and confidence bestowed on us. We also remain indebted to all those, whose contributions may not have been mentioned here in the word form, but their wishes, support and facilitation remains extremely acknowledged.

— Prof. Sanjay Singh Baghel

Brief Profile of Co-Project Director

Prof. Uma S. Singh

Prof. Uma S. Singh has been teaching at A.R.S.D. College since 1999. Presently she is the Head of the Commerce Department. She has completed her B. Com (Hons) from Shri Ram College of Commerce, M. Com and M.Phil. from Delhi School of Economics and Ph.D. from Faculty of Management Studies, University of Delhi. She has ICWAI, NET, and a Diploma in Computer Science degree. Her specialized areas are Organizational Behaviors and Human Resource Management, Business Statistics and Research Methodology. She has participated and presented papers in more than 20 national and international seminars. She is associated with many professional organizations such as TCS, Amity University, Institute of Company Secretary of India (ICSI) Delhi Chapter, Chartered Accountant of India (ICAI), Institute of Charted Financial Accountants (ICFAI), Hyderabad, IMT Ghaziabad and Stratford University USA. She is member of many esteemed organizations like Indian Association for Canadian Studies, All India Management Association (AIMA), Delhi Management association and Delhi University Commerce Association. She is having a published book title 'Management of Organizational Stress'and 'Indian Banking Industry and Eustress to her credit.

Dr. Geetanjali Batra

Geetanjali Batra is working as Associate Professor, Department of Management, Jawahar Lal Nehru University, Delhi. She has done graduation from Gargi College, University of Delhi and post-graduation from South Campus, University of Delhi. She has authored 10 papers in various international journals and presented 12 research papers at national and international conferences. Her areas of Research include Human Resource Management, Corporate Governance and Corporate Social Responsibility.

Contents

CHAPTER-I

An Overview of the social media

The human civilization has seen many radical developments since the creation of our forefathers. This quest for knowledge and desire to discover the undiscovered is what makes miraculous inventions possible. Electricity, telephone, bulb, cars, computers; as far our eyes can see, we are amazed by these inventions. Apart from the inventions, what created a stir in the way we lead our life are the ideas that these great minds harboured. These very ideas led to various revolutions that changed the world in a drastic manner. The radical revolutions in the field of science, politics, lifestyle, academics, trade; communication etc has resulted in the formation of a "global village". The saying "world is a small place" has become true because of these very revolutions.

A very significant revolution that has impacted us on a major scale is "globalization". Globalization is usually associated with liberal or free market policies in the world economy, the growing dominance of cultural life, the propagation of new information technologies and the internet revolution. The humanity stands at the threshold of realizing one single community in which major sources of social conflict have vanished. One major factor that has contributed to the easy interconnection of geographical boundaries as well as the cultural life is the internet. The World

Wide Web has the maximum impact on the creation of this vast globe turned into a global village. Social media has created a new world of social cooperation and communication due to its over-growing importance and the increasing popularity. Social media is a collection of applications based on internet fabricated on the ideological and technical fundamentals of web that enable the creation, exchange and dissemination of content generated by the user. It is a powerful means of interaction among people. Initially there were e mail chat and messenger. They have been replaced with more powerful and user-friendly social network sites such as Facebook, Orkut, Twitter, 2go, Foursquare, WhatsApp, Nimbuzz, YouTube and more lately Google+. There has been a steep rise in social networking in terms of the number of Social networking sites and their applications. The growing number of ownership and use of mobile, smart phones and tablets and the social media sites directly connected onto these devices, social networking is growing exponentially. These new social networking platforms have enormous power. There are more than two hundred social media sites out of which top 15 account for over 1.3 billion estimated visitors monthly. Facebook only had 100 million users in 2008 which increased to 1.11 Billion in 2013. Facebook launched a $5 billion IPO in February, 2012 and valued the company at $104 billion (http://www.statisticbrain.com). Over 32 million users signed up for Google+ in just 4 months of launch. Socializing is the desire to belong with another. The goal of social networking is to bring like-minded people together in order to achieve a common purpose. It's about connecting with likeminded people and allowing them to become a part of your community. Technology is important, but it will never be a substitute for community. Social networks help people grow, engages their minds, satisfies their unmet needs, and connects them to one another. These social media networks are wonderful vehicles to connect with and follow leaders of any discipline. Social media has become one of the top agenda for any business enterprise with virtually every big corporation having a Facebook or Twitter account. Facebook and Twitter have become platforms for business communication and marketing. They have enormous potential for instantly expanding connectivity. These sites have been means of popularising landmark events and movements around the world. They have been the initiators and propagators for some of the unique political and social movements that have influenced the globe in current times. Although there have been privacy concerns relating to some of the sites; but despite that, social networking has become an irreversible phenomenon.

The new generation has an extraordinary desire to connect and communicate, and the social media, devices and sites satisfy that urge of Gen-X to be seen and heard. The social networking sites have the ability to relate to the past and thus put forward connectivity. The social enthusiasts post their experiences, photographs, feelings on their walls and share them with their friends' providing foundations for sharing experiences and developing and evolving new relationships. The growth of social networking has removed the barriers of physical distance among people. The combined use of the hardware technologies and operating systems of the modern devices have made audio-visual meetings very common. The new generation believes connecting effortlessly across boundaries and oceans. The users of social networking sites are becoming communities on the basis of certain parameters of their choice. These communities are becoming popular and powerful because of their common interests and diversity. These communities are philosophically dynamic with cross-cultural and cross-functional participants. These communities are like modern age symbols of unity in diversity.

Through social media users can interact and communicate through various social links. These days millions of contemporary young users are using social media not merely to meet new people, but to grow their network in their particular field. Social networking has also helped many people in developing their identity and peer relationships. Facebook has been the most vital cause of the Egyptian Revolution that took place in 2008. Later it came to be known as the Facebook Revolution. Similarly, there are many instances, which show the various aspects where social media has made its place and has been successful at the highest rate.

There are many aspects and views to see as to how social media as a medium has helped in nation building. It helps in building a resilient nation as it involves research, usability, accessibility and provides a faster feedback mechanism. It can also be used as leverage by the government and its agencies for disaster management and emergency services. Social media such as twitter can be used as a part in engagement strategies.

Through Facebook, twitter and various other social media platforms people can show their outrage, belief, disbelief and cast their support in a more organized and systematic way. It is believed that a Nation cannot develop beyond the level at which the people of the country think. Through social media people interact with each other since it is cheaper and thereby sharing their ideas and notes and cross-fertilizing them to make the nation move in a positive and forward direction. In this research we will talk about how social media has proved to be a dynamic force in nation building which can't be avoided now.

Social networking sites which enable the people to develop their personal networking have been growing manifolds in recent years. Various studies conducted over the few years show that enjoyment followed by the number of active peers and the usefulness of the various media are the perceived benefits from the SNS. The popularity of social media is growing immensely in all walks of life. Social network sites are used by millions of people every day. With such a huge number of social communications being made and transmitted digitally, it is not surprising that researchers from fields in the sciences; both physical and social sciences have exploited this rich source of data. Facebook by its nature comprises joints between millions of users, and many concerns arise because of the number of and connections between them. Interaction is the lifeblood of human existence. It helps us to build relationships with others and with the world. Ethics guide us how we should act or behave in a particular position like professional, family, society and friends. These ethics are guidelines are to be copied and applied while interacting with the virtual world specially Facebook.

A thorough discussion will be done on the definition and meaning of social media, its origin and history, types and ethics in the subsequent pages. The focus of the study will be to understand and appreciate its contribution in the changing lifestyles and nation building and its role in Indian politics.

CHAPTER II

Social Media: Concept And Definitions

After the rapid growth of the World Wide Web, starting from the mid-90s, the revolution towards an information technology and social networking sites became a hot topic on the policy agenda for the all government and society. Yet, in this situation people of the society are not able to handle equilibrium between their private and public life.

No need to say, social media has become a global media of communication; it is a media that change the way of communication. The Advent of Social Networking Sites (SNS's) such as Facebook, Hi5, LinkedIn, netlog, google, Wayne itself is such active and humongous concept that enables its user to articulate, participate and make visible their social networks by indulging into expressing themselves in more than one way. However, no matter how big or capacious social media may be, the need to understand and work out it remains fundamentally essential as it is deemed vital to the growth of the Internet world. The internet is one of the most powerful tools used to socialize and get the chance to meet other people. It is the perfect path for people who would like to exchange concepts and ideas with people who share the same interest (Brinlee D, 2007). There were scientific studies that showed the internet as one of the fundamental tools that can initiate social interaction with other group because of the media that it employs –private and confidential. A study of new media world I have seen a lot of times how the internet, especially the social media sites are able to create a life changing situation for people. The people who are introverted and who never socialized with the peer have to found comfort with other people on the social media site because there of the feature of this social media tool to contain privacy and confidentiality. These people have learned and feel relief from the non-judgment factors. Social media sites are a better way to improve social life because rejection from people who are superficial- based, these sites were formed and built to create a means for other people to improve their social being and in the end create a new environment that is socially interactive. Prior to the existence of the social media on the web, people are accustomed to getting and acquiring the information they need through other forms such as newspapers, manual books, researchers, and other forms of literatures that were manually bound and published. These- materials are often called as the traditional forms of media. Social media is the interaction that happens and transpires between ads among people that result into essential tidbits of information employee the internet technology as the main channel of communication (Chaffey D. 2003). In a study, Researchers found there are so many social media elements, social media systems, social media relations, social media communications tools & technology, affect our daily lives. There are four type of SNS'S users.

Alpha Socializers-(a minority) people who used sites in intense shorts to flirt, meet new people, and are entertained. *Attention Seekers*- people who craved attention and comments from others, often by posting photos and customizing their profile.

Followers - peoples who joined sites to keep up what their peers were doing.

Functional- people who tended to be single minded in using sites for a particular purpose. (N.B. Ellison, C. Steinfield and C. Lampe, 2007).

Social media is the social relations among people in which they generate, share or exchange ideas and information through virtual mediums to virtual communities and networks. Andreas Kaplan and Michael Heinlein define social media as "a group of internet-based applications that on the ideological and technological foundations of web 2.0 and that allow the creation and exchange of user-generated content." Web 2.0 is described "as a platform whereby content and applications are no longer created and published by individuals, but instead are continuously modified by all users in a participatory and collaborative fashion." so Web 2.0 might be seen as the ideological and technological association of social media. The mere publishing of content is less interactive and belongs to the earlier Web 1.0 era; collaborative projects, starting with blogs, belong to Web 2.0.

Social media is based on web technologies to create a platform through which a person and communities share, discuss, and modify user generated content. The impacts comprise significant changes to communication between organizations, communities and individuals.

Social networking is defined as "the use of dedicated websites and applications to communicate with other users or to find people with similar interests to one's own". (Oxford Dictionary, 2011)

Maria-Webster dictionary the definition of social media is "forms of electronic communication through which users create online communities to share information, ideas, personal messages, and other content". Another definition includes web and mobile-based technology that encourages users to interact with each other for creating and exchanging user generated content.

Social media have evolved to include tools and practices that were not conceived of only a few years ago. Social media combines the three levels of communication. The first level is visible, and can be defined as obvious patterns and behaviours, along with technology, buildings and artefacts. The second level is less visible and involves cultural communication; that is, how people communicate both verbally and nonverbally. At the third level it is made up of the 'ideas, basic assumptions, values and beliefs held by a society' and is almost invisible. If communication can be divided into three realms of words, material things and behaviour then social media provide an interesting and complex challenge, as they bridge the three levels of culture and communication. For many people, well-known social network sites such as Facebook and Twitter typify social media. The sites have become enormously popular across demographics of race, age and gender, and have hundreds of millions of users.

CHAPTER-III

History And Evolution Of Social Media

Social media, primarily social networking sites that started from a small endeavor to stay in contact has resulted through its evolution into a huge network of sites that serves the purpose of connecting millions of individuals, groups and communities providing them a platform to discuss, share and spread their ideas. The history of social media is fascinating and essential to have a complete understanding.

In this topic we will share the very first proto-type of social media or social networking sites and gradually will move on to see the mature, evolved version of it.

In 1978, a group of Jef **Raskin** at Apple Computer Inc., Ward Christensen and Randy Suess, two members of the Chicago Area Computer Hobbyists Exchange, and employees of IBM were working to give origin to world's first social network. It all started when Christensen and Suess developed a virtual system named Dubbed CBBS **(Computerized Bulletin Board System),** where users could post public messages just like a notice board in an office. It was capable of using user's own MODEM file transfer protocol. CBBS was created to inform the group members about meetings and important announcements without placing dozens of phone calls. As more members started joining the talk and sharing information through individual postings, the early makings of a small virtual community began to emerge.

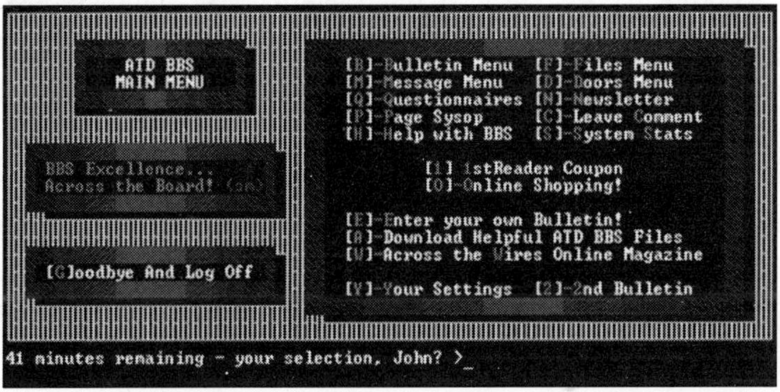

The original CBBS was the brainchild of Seuss that ran off an s-100 motherboard kit that Suess had purchased from a local market and was did not allow simultaneous users.

While CBBS didn't become very popular and only a select few could take advantage of it, another ASCII bulletin board followed its path and started popping up across a variety of platforms like Apple Net. By early 1980's Bulletin Board Systems became more standardised and streamlined due to Microsoft Disk Operating Systems. Soon, MS-DOS BBS programs by RBBS-PC and Fido developed as modem speed improved and boards started attracting more members.

Along with the growth in popularity of Bulletin Boards, they expanded in their scope. As multi-user capability became available, members began conversations with each other, replying and responding to posts. One of the earliest and popular communities was the Whole Earth Electronic Link (WELL) which was conceived in 1985 by Stewart Brands for review readers and contributors of Whole Earth to give their opinions and share their ideas with one another.

It was only with the rise of the commercial internet service providers like CompuServe, AOL, Prodigy, EarthLink that social networking as we know it today started. As Internet Service Providers provided the internet to anyone with a phone line the connectivity increased. The clubs whose membership was earlier restricted became overrun with members because of the desire for distinctiveness. Bulletin boards certainly had a unique place in the new World Wide Web, but a few sites started offering more variety to the users with a focus on establishing unique online identities.

One of the earliest and most successful of these virtual metropolises was BHI (Beverly Hills Internet). As the users of BHI increased to the tune of six million page views a month, it was given a more suitable name in late 1995, Geocities. It flourished along with Tripod, Xoom and Angelfire and by 1997 it had a population of more than a million user members.

At the same time, some of Cornell students launched theglobe.com which was similar to Geocities. It gave the users the freedom to personalize their online experiences by publishing their own content and interacting with others with similar interest.

Founders Todd Krizelman and Stephen Paternot launched their eWorld online service in 1994 inspired by the way internet was bringing together the world. It was built around a community center where ePeople would come together to meet. It was highly priced and struggled to attract members. It lasted for less than two years and hardly registered on the social networking radar.

While GeoCities, theglobe.com and eWorld were struggling to squeeze out money from their members, one new specialized service idea that immediately paid dividends was founded in 1995 by ex-Boeing exec Randal Conrads. Classmates.com was born out of a basic desire to help people regenerate their adolescence. Conrads exemplary site ignited a large number of teenagers eager to connect with old school friends. Registration was initially free, but as more and more matches were made, Classmates.com eventually adopted a payment format. It was a big success as millions of users signed up to connect with their school buddies. It also faced challenges like spam, overcharging, cancellation. All communications was routed through classmates.com servers became a pattern for future networks. Another equally successful paid site called Reunion.com (later renamed as Mylife.com) was started in 2002. It expanded classmates.com objective beyond the classroom.

As social networking was expanding its domain, a new innovation in the field of communication called instant messaging was starting. Started in 1997 by the release of AOL Instant Messenger, Instant Messenger was limited to known friends. Its system of short, rapid correspondences influenced the rise of online community.

Another social networking site, Six Degrees.com (1997-2001) became popular. After setting up the account, users having similar likes and dislikes started filling each other's rings on the basis of strength of their relationship (best friends were in the 5th degree and so on) to create a circle of friends. It was very inventive and soon became the trend, but it was based on adds for its revenues and soon became unprofitable. SixDegrees was sold in 2000 and abandoned shortly thereafter.

In March 2003, programmer Jonathan Abrams launched the first site that had many of finer points of its predecessors especially the focus on indirect relationships. Friendster made approximately three million registrants within first six months. On a path to make "friend" a verb long before Facebook hit the scene and take over a niche basically created by Friendster. Friendster would have been a household word, instead it fell victim to its own success.

As the users of Friendster increased, it became difficult for the servers to handle the traffic and thus its performance slowed down to a virtual crawl. Its founder Abram was too focused on the future and rejected a Google buyout offer of $30 million in November 2003. He had dreams of making Friendster a multi-billion-dollar enterprise.

At the same time, a small group of Los Angeles based eUniverse employees and Friendster members founded MySpace. They used their company's resources including 250 colleagues who were tasked with joining and signing up at least 10 associates. The founders Chris Dewolf and Tom Anderson had deep pockets and access to vast database. They utilized eUniverses marketing techniques to set MySpace apart from Friendster. They give users total control over content and peddling their site as a true virtual expression, musicians, celebrities, movies, TV shows, startups, presidential candidates and every adolescent with access to a computer soon joined MySpace to establish online identities.

While the founders were not able to decide on the notion of a monthly MySpace subscription fee, they ultimately decided on an ad-generation system that attached semi-obtrusive banners to individual sites; a later platform, dubbed Hyper Targeting, sharpened this model by rooting advertisers to sites based on users' specific interests. After being sold to Rupert Murdochs News Corporation in July 2005, barely two years after its founding-MySpace aggressively expanded its role as a social networker with MySpaceIM (instant messaging), MySpaceTV (video sharing), MySpace classified (personal ads) and MySpace Mobile in an attempt to keep pace with the new kid on the block who was making a lot of noise.

Facebook started with Harvard computer science Major Mark Zuckerberg's juvenile concept.

In October 2003, an inebriated Zuckerberg hacked into some of his compatriots' "face books" and set up his own site, Facemash, to compare their less-pleasing attributes in a split-screen comparison. It lasted just a few days before school administrators shut it down, but the seed was planted.

The following semester Zuckerberg gathered three of his roommates- Chris Hughes, Dustin Moskovitz and Eduardo Saverin- and set to work on creating a universal face book for Harvard students. Widely popular on campus, Zuckerberg quickly opened a Thefacebook.com to other universities (Stanford, Columbia and Yale joined first in march) and by June, the whole operation had moved to California.

Not to be contained to higher education, **Facebook** (which dropped its "The" and capitalized the "F" in August 2005) expanded to add high school networks later in 2005 and opened its doors to the rest of the world in September 2006. With a healthy buzz already brewing, a cadre of MySpace confined by their cluttered, ad-laden pages swiftly jumped ship, and by year's end some 12 million registered users were already intermingling.

Light on customization but just as heavy on content, Facebook's clean, uniform pages, instant status updates and orderly Wall of messages forever altered the landscape, and Zuckerberg's vision of a mature, sophisticated system of correspondence may have saved social networking from eventually succumbing to the next hip, young fad.

While Facebook and MySpace were dueling for supremacy, other sites eager for a piece of the expanding pie were left to fight over the scraps with an array of professional alliances, specialized clubs, cultural leagues and plain old copycats.

In 2004, Ezer Ratchaga launched his holistic personal networked called FriendCircles as a place to organize around hobbies, interests or career goals; a few months later, Tagged.com opened a site targeted to teens. By 2005, webcam junkies had Stickam and news hounds were flocking to Buzznet to share Hurricane Katrina survival stories-everyone from night clubbers to artists were given a social niche on the web.

One notable exception on the field was Bebo, a personalized blogging site launched in early 2005. An acronym for Blog Early, Blog Often, Bebo founder Michael Birch, found far greater enthusiasm for his site in his homeland of England than the United States. With an assertive overseas push (Bebo was originally based in San Francisco where his wife and Bebo co-founder, Xochi, grew up), Birch was able to hang with the big boys-and give the ubiquitous MySpace Music a run for its money- leading to an $850 million AOL buyout in march 2008.

Not one to sit on the sidelines, Google got in on the act, too. After its failed Friendster bid, the search-engine giant in 2004 unveiled Orkut (named after its creator, Orkut Bykkkten), an invitation only social network that encouraged friends to create mini groups to share related videos, pictures and ideas. Bogged down by MySpace and Facebook, the network lagged in the U.S but caught fire in Brazil and India.

Scrappy, smaller sites such as Yelp and Ning carved out their own niches, and around the world, a bevy of social networks united users while dividing and conquering the internet, including some fairly popular ones- Skyrock (France, Belgium, Switzerland);

Multiply (Philippines); mixi (Japan); Qzone (china); Badoo (2006 in Europe); Nasza klasa (Poland) but there was still a missing piece needed to bring all the pieces together.

The connection came in the form of small blue bird named **Twitter,** an instant message, micro-blogging system that tore down the unintentional barriers created by competing social networking sites. Founded in 2006, Twitter was only marginally successful until the 2007 South by southwest festival in Austin, Texas, when usage exploded, tripling to some 60,000 Tweets a day and officially entering the mainstream. A brilliant network where friends were made effortlessly and without bias and a 140-character limit ensured dialogue moved swiftly along, Twitter gave a voice to all those faces out there.

Soon, users all around the world- regardless of their choice of site-were divulging their deepest thoughts, fears and desires in rapid exchanges to as few as one and as many as million people at once. Finally, widgets added connectivity to MySpace, Facebook and virtually every social-networking web site, and tied everything and everyone- together.

What started as a note system with a dozen or so users has evolved into a global phenomenon with hundreds of millions of users reaching nearly every corner in the world. From elaborate, graphics-intensive personal pages to brief, brisk bulletins, the explosion of social networking sites has succeeded in bringing people closer together as the restless masses stand on mountaintop, waiting for the next revolution.

CHAPTER-IV

Types Of Social Media

After a long discussion on what exactly is 'social media', it has been seen that when asked from people what they mean by the term social media, it is found that most of them have a vague idea about it. The moment one speaks of social media the immediate response one gets is Facebook or twitter. However, this is a very short-sighted notion or a very limited perspective of the vast world of social media. For communicating with old friends or new ones, to making new business relationships or to reach a wider audience, social media has the ability to change the way we communicate or market ourselves online. Whether for individual, small business or big business enterprises, or even just for fun, the platter of social media offers something

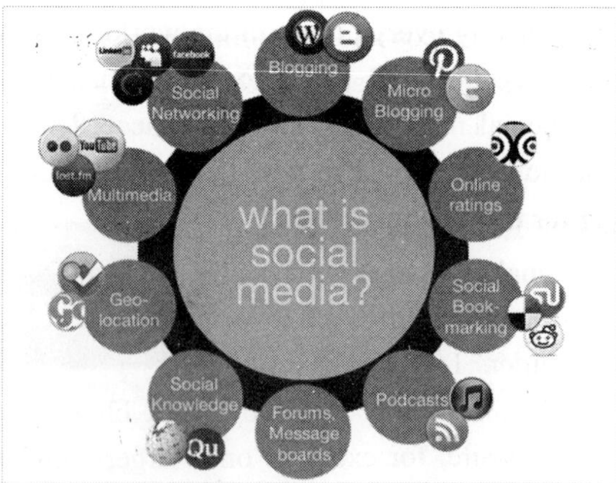

or the other for everyone. However, social media has proliferated and evolved into many new shapes and forms. This section will help you develop a deeper and wider knowledge of what is available in social media and how varied they can be.

Since the term "social media" was first introduced in 2004, the rapid changes in technologies and fragmentation into various forms of social media has been beyond belief. This evolution makes defining social media a bit slippery. Beyond that functionality and size can differ greatly. Some of the popular platforms have become a combination of these categories, however the main categories are:

Social Networks

It is one of the most popular social media categories. A social network is an online service, platform or site that allows users to have own profile and develop relationships with other users. Interaction on these platforms form online communities and people frequently share information through posts, links, photos, videos and other multimedia. Popular examples are Facebook, Google+, and LinkedIn.

Blogs

It is the earliest form of social media. It grew from personal web pages and usually displays date-stamped entries in reverse chronological order. Text-based varieties are still very popular. Short for web log, a blog is a website (or a part of a website, for example on a larger company sites) where articles are written and posted for people to read. Many blogs are written by individuals who wish to share their thoughts on a specific topic or their life in general, while others are written as multi-author collaborative efforts. Often, people can leave comments at the bottom of the blog post in order to encourage further conversation. Blogs have become very influential in modern culture and millions of people read them every day to get information and news. Popular blogging platforms include wordpress, blogger.

Microblogs

Microblog is a shorter version of a blog. It allows authors to share quick bites of information rather than long articles. These include sites like Twitter, which limits posts to 140 characters, and to posterous and tumblr.

Microblogs do not have to be text-based, for example Pinterest which mainly focuses on people sharing images or videos; and they often allow users to follow others whose posts show up on a newsfeed within the platform.

Online rating sites

While planning a trip we need information about local restaurants, must watch places, local tourist guides etc. Online rating sites like TripAdvisor, Zomato, Google allow people to leave reviews about a specific location, hotel, restaurant, etc so others can get an idea of the service providers in that area. This feature is also popular in e-commerce sites, like Amazon and eBay because people look for other's comments about products before making a purchase.

Social bookmarking

Social bookmarking sites allow users to save and share their favorite websites at a location. Users can rate these sites, tag them within categories and leave comments. Through this process, sites are recommended to others, therefore increasing visibility of the websites and helping people find content they would be interested in. Popular bookmarking sites include StumbleUpon, Del.icio.us, and Digg.

Podcasts

Podcasts are most commonly a type of audio or video file that are syndicated online for people to download or stream through a computer or mobile device. Podcasts got their name from combining "broadcasts" and "pod"- a reference to their popularity with iPod users.

Forums/message boards

Forums and message boards are one of the oldest types of social media that allow users to have a conversation about a specific topic. These sites are not usually the most advanced in functionality and design, they are still popular with people who want to ask a question or get involved with a specific conversation online. Many forums and message boards center on a general topic, question or industry. Discussions on a forum can happen under categories. Under the categories there can be sub-forums and these sub-forums can further have more sub-forums. The topics of discussion are commonly called threads. These are the places where members can start their discussions or post their comments. The discussions on forums are regulated by administrators who manage technical details on the site and moderators who manage the day to day discussions on the forum, answer queries. They have the privilege of deleting, merging, moving, and splitting locking, renaming, suspending, warning the members, adding, editing, of posts and threads.

Social knowledge/ wikis

Social knowledge sites rely on user generated content to create a central hub of knowledge for others for reference. They are platforms where people having similar interests connect with each other to tie together the scattered proficiency of the members. Some of these sites are large and can be accessed by the public, for example Wikipedia, Answers.com, and Quora, while others can be restricted to a group of people who belong to the same organization.

Geo-location

This type of social media relies on establishing the location of the user. It is usually associated with mobile devices. Geo-location platform allows users to check-in at certain locations, and find friends nearby, and get vouchers for local business. Foursquare is an example of a popular geo-location platform, while other social networks like Facebook and Google+ integrate this functionality within their larger sites.

Multimedia

Multimedia sties enable users to share videos, photos, info graphics, and PDFs rather than text. People can usually leave comments and share the content with others. Popular examples include YouTube, Instagram, last.fm and slideshare.

Each of the Social media sites have a different purpose. Individuals can choose what is best suitable for them and rejoice in the vast scope of social media.

Development of a systematic classification scheme for social media is difficult, as new sites appear every day. Social media can be classified on the basis of social presence and media richness on the one hand, and self-presentation and self-disclosure on the other.

To demonstrate, they have combined the two classifications into a table that illustrates their arguments (Table 1.1)

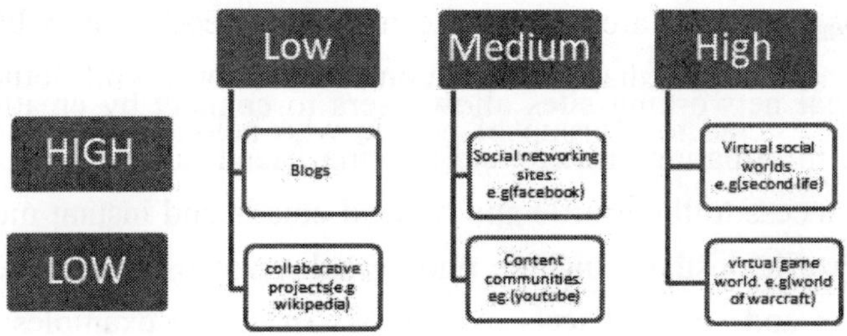

Table 1.1: classification of goals for social media.

The table shows how different types of social media involve different commitments from the user. For example, a person who wishes to become a fully involved user in a virtual social world, rather than merely adding daily textual additions to their blog, would in a general sense disclose more about themselves (whether consciously or not), and their online presence would necessarily require a more involved use of media tools. **Kaplan and Haenlein's** categorization of social media is adopted here to enable discussion about the various types:

Collaborative projects

Some social networking sites like Wikipedia enable the joint and simultaneous creation of content by many users. Some of these sites allow users to add, remove and change content; others form of 'social bookmarking', in that they allow the group-based collection and rating of internet links or media content.

·Content communities

Main purpose of content communities is the sharing of media content between users, including text (e.g. Bookcrossing), photographs (Flickr), videos (YouTube) and PowerPoint presentations (Slide Share). Users are not usually required to create a personal profile page.

Social networking sites allow users to connect by creating personal information profiles and inviting friends and colleagues to have access to the profile and to send emails and instant messages. Profiles usually include photographs, videos, audio files, and blogs and so on. Facebook and MySpace are examples of social networking sites.

Virtual game worlds

Virtual game worlds replicate a three-dimensional environment in which users appear in the form of personalized avatars and interact according to the rules of the game. They have gained popularity with the support of devices such as Microsoft's XBox and Sony's PlayStation. An example is World of Warcraft. Virtual worlds allow inhabitants to choose behavior more freely and to live (in the form of avatars) in a virtual world similar to their real life. An example is Second Life.

This was an overview of the various broad categories that can be used to differentiate among the different types of social media.

- Twitter – Being a micro blogging site, allows users to broadcast short posts/tweets.

- Linked in – A site basically for the professional community. The members establish, document and share their network with people whom they trust professionally.
- Reddit – Stories are promoted by the site members called redditors. Consisting of many subreddits which includes many topics. Main goal is to promote topics which have been voted more.
- YouTube – A video sharing site, allows users to upload, share, subscribe , watch videos

CHAPTER V

Some Popular Social Networking Sites

There has been a sharp rise in the number and types of social networking sites available and the variety of services that they offer. This chapter reviews some of the popular social networking sites like FACEBOOK, YOUTUBE, LINKEDIN, TWITTER, GOOGLE+, Hi5, MySpace, NING, XING, Friendster, TUMBLR, Classmates, VINE, Meetup, Ask.fm, WhatsApp, Viber, WeChat.

Facebook

Facebook, founded on February 4, 2004, by Mark Zuckerberg with his college roommates and fellow is an online social networking service with its headquarters in Menlo Park, California. Its membership was initially offered to Harvard students, but later extended to Boston area colleges, the Ivy League, and Stanford University. Further its added students at numerous other universities and afterwards extended it to high-school students. Facebook now allows anyone who is at least 13 years old worldwide to become its registered user, although proof is not required. After registering, users may create a individual profile, connect with friends, add other users as friends, exchange and share their ideas and messages, post status updates and photos, and receive notices when others update their profiles, share pictures, send messages and keep in touch with everyone.

Users can connect with the groups of people who are having common interest, workplace, school or college, and categorize their friends into lists such as "People From Workplace" or "Close Friends circle". Facebook had its initial public offering in February 2012 and started selling stock to the public three months later accomplishing a pinnacle market capitalization of $104.

Facebook is the most popular social networking site of all time. The popularity of Facebook has increased drastically. Within 6 years Facebook has reached more than 1 billion users and still growing rapidly. Nowadays Facebook has become status simple of our life. It is helping us in various ways and also harming us in some other different ways. The use of Facebook could be very helpful if any kind of addiction is avoided.

USEs

- Facebook is a absolutely free and one of the best medium for communication. It can be use to post messages, start a video call, and upload pictures and videos for free.
- Facebook facilitates to connect with different people from across the world, as almost majority of the people is familiar with Facebook today. This provides us the opportunity to know more about their culture, rituals, custom, values and tradition.
- Facebook offers an email address to receive email outside of Facebook such as, Yahoo, Gmail, outlook and Hotmail. The email address is given based on the username of the

Facebook ID. One can also receive files attachment through Facebook email.

- Business organisations are using Facebook advertising and Fan pages for successful marketing campaign.
- Students are using to connect with their peer group for group study by creating a Facebook group not only for studying, but they can share any kind of information about projects, homework, assignments, exams, due date etc.
- Facebook plays a very important role in getting latest valuable information. Facebook fan pages and users are constantly sharing many valuable news and information.

Youtube

There are lots of video-sharing sites on the web, but YouTube is the one that captures the first place. It is by far the site with the highest number of users both viewers and up loaders and the maximum traffic. Marketer, are also using YouTube as one of the social media marketing tool.

However, marketing in YouTube also has its fair share of pros and cons.

1. Easy to Share

Below each video, there are sharing options users can easily click on to make your video viral. They can Like the video, recommend it to their network in Twitter, Facebook or send the video through e-mail to their friends. Leveraging on social media sites maximizes your video sharing capacity. To boost the promotion, post your YouTube video links onto bulletin boards of your friends. In this way, their visitors will also see the link on their friend's profile. When they get interested, your video gets another unique view count and you have an added chance to have a new subscriber.

2. FREE

Your uploaded YouTube videos will appear in both YouTube and Google search engines. You can get your brand go viral with millions of views, introduce your company and the benefits of your products—all without cost. There are no fees to pay in using YouTube. So don't worry if you're just starting out and experimenting on its use. You can practice and test your own creative ways on doing videos and see how the market reacts for free.

3. Strategic Tagging

Alexa ranks YouTube as the second highest trafficked site globally. What this means is that when you market your products and services through YouTube videos, you can have about 60 million viewers in a month. Emarketer says that the market is predominately Generation Y online surfers who understand 18 languages. They explore the Internet about five to six hours daily. Given this demographics, you can have a smarter way of knowing who and how to target them.

Linkedin

LinkdIn is a social network created for professional networking.

LinkedIn has over 75 million members worldwide. What's great about using LinkedIn is that unlike some other social networking websites, all profiles are career or business oriented. This has several advantages.

Professional Image: Because LinkedIn is for professional networking, you won't see photos of someone's vacation, graduation or get party invitations posted in your profile timeline. Not that these things aren't important, but if a potential employer or client views your profile, you want them to have a strictly professional image of you.

Networking: LinkedIn allows you to build your professional network in several ways. You and your LinkedIn connections may have the same career focus, work in the same industry, be a member of the same associations, reside in the same city, or reside anywhere in the world. Professional connections can be very helpful when searching for a new position, building your client base, or finding business partners.

Career Opportunities: LinkedIn profiles can be used as on-line resumes. Many recruiters are now turning to LinkedIn to search for potential employees based on the work experience, education, and credentials listed in LinkedIn profiles. In addition, LinkedIn allows you to upload a resume if you'd like. It also allows you to indicate if you are interested in job opportunities or not. So if you're not interested in talking to recruiters, they'll see that in your profile.

Associations: Many associations are now using LinkedIn as a social networking tool for their members. They use LinkedIn to communicate news, events, and other important information to their members. Associations often send out weekly newsletters to its LinkedIn group members to keep them up-to-date with current events and sometimes notifying them of current job openings that may be of interest.

Professional Resources: There are many career, education, and community related groups you can join on LinkedIn.Groups can be used as a resource to ask questions, find answers, give advice, share information, take polls, and much more.

Twitter

There are lots of success stories and case studies that document the success businesses have had through Twitter. Here are a few of my favorite ways to use the social network for new business benefits.

1. Monitor real-time conversations

Use Twitter search and other simple listening tools to monitor real-time conversations about your brand. This will help your marketing and management teams see what people are really saying about your company. There are a variety of free and effective listening tools available that allow you to save searches, such as Tweetdeck and HootSuite. One heating and air-conditioning company had its best year ever simply because it monitored tweets about broken home systems and offered prompt help.

2. Extend customer service

A lot of companies and organizations use Twitter as a form of customer service. You can find many well-documented best practices if you do an Internet search on the topic. When people "call" your company on Twitter, do you pick up the phone?

3. Offer helpful links and headlines

Drive traffic to your website, blog, landing pages, YouTube channels, Facebook, etc., when you offer helpful links and headlines in your tweets. Despite the hype about social media, websites are still important in the social information eco-system. Your website is usually the place where you ask for money—registrations, downloads, or whatever you're selling.

4. Catch problems early

Twitter can help you discover consumer problems, product issues, or potentially damaging PR disasters before they cause trouble. Pick up conversations about your company and respond quickly.

5. Break through communication barriers with tweets

If you have a hard time making business connections with cold calls and email, try a tweet or direct message. You will not believe how well this works. People may not return calls, but they almost always return tweets. I don't know the psychology behind this, but I know it works.

6. Run special deals and promotions

Special deals and promotions on Twitter can drive traffic or move slow-moving stock. If you've done a good job surrounding yourself with targeted connections, they should be interested in your specials, right?

A local bakery can use this idea to move its products if it baked too much of a certain item that day. Here's an example tweet: "Come by before 4 p.m. for 2 for 1 coffee cakes." In my opinion, coffee cake qualifies as meaningful content!

GOOGLE+

Google+ Search

The search engine integration opportunities speak for themselves, as demonstrated in this search advertisement example. Google reports that Search ads using Google+ average 5-10% more clicks – consumers trust the addition of the +1 button in ads and on sites. Authorship capabilities through Google+ also increase content credibility. When it comes to establishing a strategy on Google+, it's important to take advantage of the longer post allowances. This enables you to include more relevant brand keywords and phrases that will aid in SEO efforts. This ties in greatly with Local SEO as well – Google+ Local is the integration of Google Search, Google+ Social and Google Maps.

97% of consumers search for local businesses online. Google+ Local offers countless benefits for businesses, including an optimized profile highlighted on the right-hand side of Google search results. We explain exactly what to expect from a Google+ profile and local reviews here.

Google+ Social

Of course, Google+ (G+) is also a well-known social network, meaning that engagement is a key metric. +1's are the goal – they're how users express interest or appreciation (the Google version of a "like"). Comments and shares are also vital, and necessitate high-quality content.

All of those metrics are reached by way of understanding the network demographics. Just as you wouldn't post a tweet on Facebook and expect social success, your content must be altered to fit G+. It's a more educational community, somewhere between Facebook and LinkedIn. Roughly 67% of the G+ audience is male, with the average user being a "techie" in his late twenties.

Hi5

Hi5 started its social networking service in 2003. It has shifted its focus over the years, starting with social networking, moving to gaming and finally becoming a dating social networking site.

- Hi5 is designed to help you make new friends. You can choose to see status updates from your group of friends or from everyone who uses it. Not only that, but you can filter the updates you see to be only from a certain gender, age range, country and city. This specific filtering gives you an advantage that few other social network sites have – you can see if there is anything fun or worthwhile to do locally.
- You can customize your hi5 page with skins created by other users. However, once you choose a skin, you cannot customize it farther with HTML or CSS code. You can also use the simple profile editor that allows you to change background color, font types and sizes. The profile page allows you to post details about yourself such as your physical description, who you are looking to network with and where you are from.

- There is a Privacy link at the top of every page where you can adjust a number of privacy settings, including who sees your profile, accepting comments, and message and photo settings. Hi5 allows you to be specific when setting your privacy options. Each major section of your profile can have its own privacy setting, such as friends only, all users, tagging photos and more.

MySpace

MySpace or short for myspace.com is a social networking website and is one of the largest online communities available today. MySpace is a world in itself and it brings together various races, occupations, orientations and social classes together making a powerful group to interact with each other.

The advantages of using MySpace are many and a few of them are listed here:

- **Meeting people from across the globe:** MySpace is a collection of people from all across the world and includes people from various professions, races, cultures and religions. It thus opens up a lot of vistas to get to know new people and network with old friends and acquaintances who are unreachable. This kind of networking and interaction encourages people to improve their understanding and knowledge base with respect to regions and cultures across the globe.

- Cultural learning: All of us grow up in a singular culture normally inculcated by our parents and family. As a result, we are not knowledgeable about other cultures that exist. MySpace puts members in touch with diverse cultures and religions thus improving understanding and knowledge. This is done on MySpace through discussions and chats that are a part of its culture.
- Connecting offline: Due to MySpace befriending a lot of connections come face to face in real life resulting in great interaction and traditional networking. Although MySpace integrates communities across the world, it is easy to find friends in one's own geographical area. If a member is a traveler, having friends at different geographical areas is a distinct advantage for securing information as well as social company.
- Building businesses: Although MySpace is a social platform it is a great tool to network for building business, especially those that involve multi-level marketing. Moreover, getting to know people from various countries encourages professional relationships in the form of partnerships and representation to build and expand businesses geographically.
- Multimedia: A lot of multimedia features are available all across MySpace and what is more interesting is that they can be used for free on member's websites. Contributing to this collection can be fun and interesting.
- Editing: MySpace profile is highly customizable and a member can add almost anything to it using Java and HTML editing features.

- Communication: MySpace offers a variety of communication features to its member that include email, instant messaging, forums, blogs, groups and bulletin boards that can be used to keep in touch with friends and family at almost no cost at all.

NING

Ning is an online service that allows users to create their own social networks and join and participate in other networks. Ning lets creators of networks determine the site's appearance and functionality, as well as whether the site is public or private. Most networks include features such as photos or videos, lists of network members and events, groups within the network, and communication tools such as forums or blogs. No technical skill is required to set up a social network, and there are no limits to the number of networks a user can join. Ning offers no-cost networks, which are supported by advertisements, or users can pay for premium services that eliminate ads and let users choose network URLs that are separate from the Ning domain.

When it comes to advantages, Ning has several of them:

Firstly, it is completely free. A social network around a website or blog is a great thing to have. It helps interact more with your blog's readers. You can have forums for your users to post comments, suggestions, or queries; you can have the blog feature to have your users to share their blog entries; and you can pretty much promote your blog through this social network.

Hence, it is great to have a good social network around your blog. If you have a good loyal readership, then consider creating a social network at Ning.

XING

Xing was initially established as Open Business Club AG in August 2003 in Germany by Lars Hinrichs and Bill Liao. The name was changed to Xing in November of 2006. Over the next several years, it merged with social networking businesses in Spain, Turkey, and Italy. The Xing platform is a social and business networking tool for professionals. Over eight million people use Xing in one of the sixteen languages currently available. The site has approximately 150,000 unique visitors each month.

Xing's main competitor is LinkedIn. Both offer similar services and platforms, although LinkedIn's service offers more access to non-paying members. Xing attracts more small businesses and independent business owners than its competitors.

Xing is an application that may be used for networking between business professionals. Similar to LinkedIn, Xing users can enter relevant business and professional information and connect with others with similar interests. Building a network of business professionals worldwide is the main purpose of the application.

Friendster

There are many social media sites such as Facebook and Twitter and Friendster.com fits in this category. A lot of social networking goes on among people; especially friends, families, school or any social groups, interest and activity groups who share common views and interests. Friendster boasts of over 110 millions who use it to interact with one another on the internet, making it one of the leading social networking outfits.

Social networking forums like Friendster can actually be beneficial to web marketers if it is used well to enable people promote relationships. It is recommended that if you want to always be on the Friendster, try to promote products or sites and issues that are popular with other members. You need to be frank and down to earth, in order to reap the full benefits of being on this social network forum.

To benefit more on the Friendster, try the following useful ideas.

Be real- Do not try to fake it on this forum, just talk frankly about your exploits and disappointments.

Chat- The Chat section will enable you to talk about topics of interest, sharing your views freely with those present online through Friendster.com. Just picture yourself chatting to thousands of friends in one chat room, and see what a goldmine this can be to those who want to improve their social relationships.

Avoid selling- Suffice it to say that this is a social network forum and not a trading link. You will only succeed if you stick to the issues and products that other members take interest in.

Be helpful and friendly- Allow others to say their bit and then add your own views in order to promote the general good and help others achieve their goals.

Remain invested- It takes pretty hard work and long periods to build a fan base. Just having a small fraction visiting regularly will send traffic flowing in to your website little by little so keep on working hard at it. You will see the traffic increasing in your website, with the more trust people have in you and it will take time. Eventually this will translate into a higher conversion rates for those products you sell.

Tumblr

Tumblr is a very popular place for people who want to set up blogs. There is of course a reason that it is so popular. That reason has to do with the fact that it has a lot of benefits over other blogging sites. Once you know what these benefits are you will likely want to use Tumblr as well.

- The main benefit of Tumblr is that it is really easy to use. It does not require that you have any technical skills in order to be able to start blogging. It has a very easy user interface that most people can figure out in a matter of minutes at which point all you have to do is start writing whatever you want on your blog. One of the other benefits is that unlike most other blogging sites they don't worry too much about the length of your posts so if you want to have a post that is just a couple of sentences long that is an option.
- Another huge benefit of using Tumblr is that you can customize it to meet your needs. One of the problems with

most blogging sites is that you have no choice over how the blog looks. If you are using the blog for business you are going to want it to look similar to your website, this is something that you can do with Tumblr. Even more importantly you can have a custom domain on Tumblr which means that you are not required to use one of those awkward subdomains that you have to use on most other blogging sites. You can have a domain that people will remember and associate with your company.

- Tumblr also offers the huge advantage of having a built in source of traffic. It is not just a blogging site but it is a whole community. That means that people will go to their home page and use it as a way to find blogs that they are interested in. This will really help to bring in a lot of traffic that you would otherwise not get. In addition because of all the links that will point at your blog from the other pages on Tumblr you will find that your blog tends to rank a lot better in the search engines which brings in even more traffic.

Classmates

The website facilitates member's search, meet and keep relation with fellows and relatives all the time. It has more than 40 million members in the United States and Canada and its traffic is ranked at 500 by Alexa.com.

There is no cost for users to create logins as a user of Classmates.com. As a user you may also attach/upload picture, messages, life time history.

Gold membership can be obtained by paying nominal charges through credit or debit card, they can also send emails to any user, can use website facilities for programming get together and celebrations, and can create personal groups and can use my network to keep in touch with friends.

Classmates.com users use initial names, not dummy names. Users personal information is secure with double-blind email system, so email ID and personal data are never viewed till self-disclosed by users one-on-one. Feature of classmates.com are privacy, ownership ,business models, business practice references and external links.

Vine

Vine is a mobile app that allows to capture videos from your mobile device in short, six-second looping videos. These short videos can than be shared with your Twitter followers and Facebook friends.

To Engage Your Followers in Conversation, start a conversation with your followers using a Vine video. Highlight Your Brand Advocates. It can be used for advertising one of your products on a Vine video? Vine displays your work for a client so that ther is no static portfolio on your website. Offer the users relevant historical details. Not everything has to be about business. General Electric shares some historical trivia related to their industry that their fans might find interesting.

Get People Excited About a New Product: Sometimes visual inspiration can really get people excited about a new product you have in the works. Vine may be used to give fans a preview of their upcoming video game package.

Educate and Amaze: Anytime you have the chance to educate your audience with something fascinating.

Promote a Contest: Sometimes businesses find it hard to get their fans excited about contests, because unless fans are also customers, they may not know enough about your product to know they want it.

Meetup

Meetup was formed in 2002. It is an online social networking site. People from all over the world can share their common interest with others and meet offline through Meetup. User has to enter zip code or city and the topic for discussion. The topics for discussion range from books, beauty, games, politics, health, business, jobs, pets, shopping, and technology. The time and venue of meeting will be arranged by the organizers of the group. In case user is not sure about topic of discussion user can choose from the topic listed after entering the location.

We see that Meetup has easily segregated people in different groups. This segregation can help any marketer to reach it potential or existing client by way of Meetup.

For example, maybe your company manufactures beauty products in New Zealand. Then your company can join Meetup and be a member of a group consisting of people of New Zealand, who are interested in discussing beauty-related topics. Furthermore, you also have the option to join a group with people from all over the world interested in beauty product. After joining the group you can have discussions about the product of your company with the members and invite them to an event to network and distribute your product as a sample.

Ask.fm

The social media website Ask.fm has recently sparked controversy across the country, especially in high schools. Ask.fm is a popular social networking site with over 60 million registered users. The website allows individuals to ask other users question either anonymously or as an identified user. Though many use Ask.fm to entertain themselves, critics say that it can easily be used as an instrument of cyber bullying. However, Ask.fm is a useful social tool because it allows people to find out what others think about them and build upon flaws after hearing constructive criticism through the anonymity of the site.

With Ask.fm, one can get to know more about people from other social groups, classes and grades by their answers. This tactic can be used to clear up rumors, get to know a person's interests, find out about a person's thoughts and stances on issues, etc. Also, individuals can tell others their honest opinions of them. In return, users get a chance to find out what their peers think about them via the questions and statements asked.

Ask.fm allows people to ask questions or write comments without social consequences. Since one does not need an account to write messages to other people, it is nearly impossible to figure out who wrote what unless the asker decides to reveal his or her username. This aspect takes away the face-to-face judgment and discomfort that comes with an unusual question. In school days especially, where cliques and judgment are plentiful, it can be difficult to approach someone outside of one's "normal" social group.

WhatsApp

WhatsApp Messenger is an instant messaging service available in smart phones and some selected feature phones. It uses the internet for communication. Other then text messages, users can send messages, images, video, or audio/media messages as well as their current position. WhatsApp Inc. was founded in 2009 by US citizens Brian Acton and Jan Koum. Both are former employees of Yahoo. It is situated in Mountain View, California. Facebook Inc. has taken over WhatsApp Inc. on February 19, 2014, for US$19 billion. As of 22 April 2014, WhatsApp had over 500 million monthly active users, 700 million photos, 100 million videos and more than 10 billion messages each day. Later on WhatsApp was switched from a free to paid service to control the users and cover the cost of sending verification texts to their users. In December 2009 WhatsApp can be uploaded in iPhone and can be send updated information and photos to their friends and family.

A major privacy and security problem is that WhatsApp requires users to upload their mobile phone's entire address book to WhatsApp servers. Thus WhatsApp could discover who, among the users' contacts, is available via WhatsApp. While this is a fast and convenient way to quickly find and connect the user with contacts who are also using WhatsApp, it means that their address book including contact information for contacts who are not using WhatsApp will be mirrored on the WhatsApp servers.

On March 31, 2013, the telecommunications authority of Saudi Arabia, the Communications and Information Technology Commission (CITC), issued a statement regarding possible measures against WhatsApp, among other applications, unless the service providers took serious steps to comply with monitoring and privacy regulations. A user does not need to send a friend request to send messages to another user. However, users can block numbers on WhatsApp. A public corporation of the state of Schleswig-Holstein has advised against using WhatsApp, as the service lacks privacy protection such as end-to-end client side encryption technology. On February 19, 2014, Facebook announced it would be obtaining WhatsApp for US$19 billion, in what will be its largest procurement to date. "Facebook, who was recommend by Allen & Co, will pay $4 billion in cash, $12 billion in Facebook shares and an additional $3 billion in restricted stock units to be granted to WhatsApp's founders (advised by Morgan Stanley), Jan Koum, Brian Acton,[40] and employees that will vest over four years subsequent to closing". The transaction is the largest purchase of a company backed by venture capitalists ever. The deal happened only months after a venture capital financing round valued the business at almost $1.5 billion. Just days after the announcement, WhatsApp users experienced a loss of service, leading to anger across social media.

The acquisition of WhatsApp by Facebook was not foreseen, but only weeks before the acquisition Facebook changed the approvals in the Facebook app for Android. The Facebook app needed access to the text-messages in the phone from that moment on.

The achievement caused a considerable amount of users to move, or try out other message services as well. Telegram claimed to have seen 8 million additional downloads of its app. Line claimed to have seen 2 million new users for its service. Also many other messenger applications & services saw a growth of users such as TextSecure, Blackberry Messenger and Viber. WhatsApp not only experienced an exodus of users, but also gained lots of new operators due to the media attention in regions where WhatsApp is not so well known yet.

At the Mobile World Congress in Barcelona in February 2014, Facebook CEO Mark Zuckerberg said that Facebook's gaining of WhatsApp was closely associated to the Internet.org vision. According to a TechCrunch article, Zuckerberg's vision for Internet.org was to grow a group of basic internet services that would be free of charge to use. These could be a social networking service like Facebook, a messaging service, maybe search and other things like meteorological conditions. Providing a bundle of these free of charge to users will work like a gateway drug of sorts – users who may be able to have the funds for data services and phones these days just don't see the point of why they would pay for those data services. This would give them some context for why they are important, and that will lead them to paying for more services like this – or so the hope goes.

"Competing with a number of Asian-based messaging services (like LINE, WeChat, Telegram), WhatsApp moved ten billion messages per day in August 2012, growing from two billion in April 2012, and one billion the previous October. On June 13,

2013, WhatsApp said that they had reached their new daily record by processing 27 billion messages". In April 2014, WhatsApp crossed half-a-billion user mark. As of May 2014, Whatsapp has crossed 50 million monthly active operators in India, which is also its biggest country by the number of monthly active users.

Viber

Viber is an instant messaging voice-over-Internet Practice application for smartphones established by Viber Media. In addition to text messaging, users can share images, videos and audio vedio messages. The user software is accessible for Mac OS, Android, BlackBerry OS, iOS, Series 40, Symbian, Bada, Windows Phone, and Microsoft Windows. Viber works on both 3G/4G and Wi-Fi networks. It first requires installation on a phone in order to work on a desktop functioning system environment. Viber has over 100 million monthly active users from its 280 million global registered users. Viber was initially launched for iPhone on December 2, 2010, in direct struggle with Skype. A pre-release version for Humanoid appeared in May 2011 but was restricted to 50,000 users; an unrestricted version was released on July 19, 2012. Viber for BlackBerry and Windows Phone devices was launched on May 8, 2012. On reaching 90 million users on July 24, 2012, group messaging service and HD Voice engine were added to both Android and iPhone applications. Applications for Nokia's Series 40, Symbian and Samsung's Bada platform were also announced on the same day. Initially, the voice calling feature was only available for iPhone and Android applications, with a promise that voice would be added in upcoming forms for Bada, Symbian and Windows Phone applications, with no mention of either Series 40 or Blackberry OS. The limitation seems to lie in core of Blackberry OS and Series 40 which does not have easy support for VoIP apps. As promised, on September 22, 2012, HD quality phone calls and hold group-messaging sessions were made available for Windows phone but only for Nokia users as part of exclusive partnership with Nokia. Viber with voice was officially released for all Windows Phone 8 devices on April 2, 2013. In August 2013, Viber for Linux was released as a public beta. Initially, only 64bit binaries were made available for download. On February 13, 2014, Rakuten announced they had acquired Viber for $900 million.

There was a case for intellectual property from Microsoft due to Skype in market. The actual functionality varies from platform to platform with iOS and Android being the first to receive new features. Viber includes text, picture and video messaging across all platforms, with voice calling available only to iPhone, Android and Microsoft's Windows Phone although HD voice is planned for Windows Phone 8. The application's user interface includes tab bar on the bottom giving access to messages, recent calls, contact, the keypad and a button for accessing more options. Upon installation, it creates a user account using one's phone number as username. Viber synchronizes with the phone's address book, so users do not need to add contacts in a single book. Since all users are registered with their phone number, the software returns all Viber users among one's contacts. The newest version of Viber (Version 2.3) has added smileys and other default images.

As of December 2013, Viber officially launched Viber Out, a feature that allows users the option to call mobile and land-line numbers; thus Viber users can call people not using a Viber app. Viber Out was originally released in November only to help Typhoon Haiyan victims in the Philippines connect with their valued ones. To use the new feature, users have to visit the "More" tab and choose Viber Out. No update is needed for the feature

WeChat

The app is available on Android, iPhone, BlackBerry, Windows Phone and Symbian phones, and there are also Web-based and OS X clients but these require the user to have the app installed on a supported mobile phone for authentication. As of 2013, WeChat has 300 million users; with 70 million outside China. WeChat provides text messaging, hold-to-talk voice messaging, broadcast (one-to-many) messaging, sharing of photographs and videos, and location sharing. It can exchange contacts with people nearby via Bluetooth, as well as provided that several features for contacting people at casual if desired (if these are open to it) and addition with social networking services such as those run by Facebook and Tencent QQ. Photographs may also be inflated with filters and captions, and a machine translation service is available. Registration is completed through Facebook Connect, email, mobile phone SMS/VM, or Tencent QQ. WeChat is being encouraged in India via gaming site Ibibo, in which Tencent holds a stake. WeChat began as a project at Tencent Guangzhou Research and Project center in October 2010. The original name of the app, "Weixin", was invented by Xiaolong Zhang, and named by Ma Huateng, Tencent CEO. WeChat currently is free to download and use. In May 2013, it was revealed that Rainie Yang would be a product endorser for WeChat. To promote the app in India, WeChat recruited Bollywood actors Varun Dhawan and Parineeti Chopra as brand ambassadors. On 5 August 2013, WeChat 5.0 was launched with new features and functions including payment center, games center and sticker shop. In June 2014, Wechat closed 20 million accounts because they offered prostitution services. According to GlobalWebIndex, WeChat is the fifth most used Smartphone application worldwide.

CHAPTER-VI

Growing Popularity Of Social Media

Social media considered as way of communication, interactions among people in which they can create, share, and exchange information and ideas in virtual communities and networks. Social media distinguished from traditional media to new media in many ways such as feasibility, quality, reach, frequency, immediacy and permanence. There are many effects that shoot for internet usage. It plays an important role in teenagers / youth life. There are countless of social networking sites that have created broad connections among teens. For example, Facebook, Instagram, Twitter, Skype, YouTube, and the like are used quite frequently. Social media helps teens stay connected to each other even if they are a thousand miles away, and it keeps us up to date with what's going on around the world and so on. Social media assists to strengthen relationships among youth; likeminded people have friends and fraternity. Who they didn't meet since school, or who have moved away, and they want to stay connected with. Now, they don't have to worry about losing relationship. Through social media not only teenagers can stay connected with friends but in any age individual can maintain relationship to anybody. No matter the distance or time. Just by simply sending a friend request and accepting it, then start a chat you can be back in touch again. Whether, they are known or strangers. Social networks have offers individuals with the opportunity to connect with others and build better associations with friends with whom we are incapable to meet face-to-face, and letting them be acquainted with about our life and take input about their lives and day to day happening with them.

It's very essential to understand what's going on around us rather than just knowing what's happening with friends. Today younger generation's individuals receive digital news from social media sites rather than turning on news channel or reading newspaper. 70% of youths obtain most of the news stories they read or watch via Facebook or Twitter. It's remarkable how fast news spread on social networking sites one corner to another corner. For Twitter users, though, the news links come from a more even mix of family and friends and news organizations. Majority of these users also feel that without Twitter, they would have missed this kind of news. Consequently, social media results in teens being more knowledgeable and educated about national and global news than they would be otherwise.

Social media has become indispensable of the modern youth's lifestyle. It makes our life so much easier, comfortable and much more efficient. It has become an important part of our communication culture that cannot be taken away easily, because we are so dependent on it.

It also gives people a chance to express themselves in ways that some many disapprove of in public places such as school, where people get judged by students or people who don't let you express yourself like TEACHERS, because if someone was to judge you on Facebook, twitter, etc. you can always deleted them which many can't do in their lives outside of social media. It can also build self-esteem, if someone doesn't like who they are outside of social media they can always change that and become and new person. For someone who is shy around people, in person, can also be a social butterfly online, which can also give them the confidence to be like that in person and not be shy. Many YouTube users that are now internet famous got bullied and teased because of who they were, but they found something they love to do and stopped being the one that no one liked and started to be someone everyone LOVES. Social media can be a way out for many people who struggle in life, have no friends, or aren't as social as everyone else. It gives them a chance to meet new people and find friends which they couldn't have done due to being shy and or nervous. Parents and teachers think all this bad stuff about social media, but behind closed doors it's really changing people's lives.

Social networking sites provide a platform to people to interact using the internet. Social media diminishes geography, economizes time, demolishes hierarchy and erases identity. It is the fastest way of communication. One can also share photos, videos and audios by just a click. It provides a vehicle for visual communications cutting across borders and is a good measure of expressing love and affection like parents communicating with children abroad or siblings settled across the globe.

Social media is also used as a source of recreation. Many people derive a sense of pleasure from the use of social media. Social networking sites are mostly blue in colour, and this has a psychological reasoning behind it. The colour blue is said to have a calming effect on the human brain. Hence, many users also derive a sense of enjoyment by spending time on such sites. It provides a medium through which one is constantly connected with friends and family instilling a sense of security and belonging. Facebook, one of the most popular social networking sites, also known as the Social Capital of the internet offers the same advantages. One can look for the people they know and can 'friend' them by just a click. It offers features such as the news feed which keeps the user updated about the movement of their 'friends'. One can update his status, upload photos, join groups and also play games on Facebook. The new and much hyped social networking sites are a frontier that is rich with opportunities, threats and risks. It is majorly a platform to perform various tasks like instant messaging profoundly known as email, downloading songs, posting pictures. With the positive impacts come the negatives too, thus one must constantly keep a tab of what one is posting online. Social Media has in the recent years gained a lot of importance, people use it to socialize, gather information almost for 30 years (Carton, S. (2009)).

Social networking sites which enable the people to develop their personal networking have been growing manifolds in recent years. SNS provide a new method of communicating employing computers as a collaborative tool to accelerate group formation and escalate the scope and influence of the group (Kane, Fichman, Gallaugher, & Glaser, 2009; Pfeil, Arjan, & Zaphiris, 2009; Ross et al., 2009). New developments in technology have made internet accessible to a wider population. People all over the world are now sustaining relationships with others through various social networking sites like Facebook, twitter, MySpace etc. SNS have infiltrated lives of many with amazing rapidity to become an important platform in computer related communication. These social media sites let those who are on it make profiles of themselves where they can add pictures, statuses and other personal information and share it with people via various applications and groups on the internet. In this information age, these SNS' are making young adults their main targets. Many of them use social media networks to communicate with family, friends, and even strangers. Social media sites have formed for non-personal ways of relations and young adults have taken benefit of this technological movement. Social media influenced college student's communication with others and their own self-concept.

MySpace was launched to compete with various sites like Friendster, Xanga etc. According to co-founder Tom Anderson, the founders wanted to attract the abandoned Friendster users. After rumors begun that Friendster would generate a new fee system where the site would no longer be free of charge, users posted Friendster messages inviting people to join alternate SNSs like Tribe.net and MySpace. Due to this MySpace was able to enlarge exponentially as Friendster left its users lynching in the middle. Further, MySpace made its page very user friendly as it kept adding various features on its pages according to the suggestions it gathered from its users. Thus, MySpace used all the shortcomings of Friendster to build up a whole community of active users and thus popularized very quickly. As teens began using the site rather vigorously, the site encouraged and invited their friends and acquaintances to join it rather than rejecting naïve and underage users. MySpace allowed minors also as users. As the site grew, the main featured users included the artists, the teens (including minors) and the college youth. Due to the paucity of wide media coverage during 2004, few others noticed the site's growing popularity. MySpace was purchased by News Corporation for $580 million in July, 2005 attracting huge amount of media attention. Thereafter, MySpace was accused of various safety issues. The site was blamed to host a lot of sexual interactions between adults and minor causing a great deal of legal action. A major concern relating to sexual pedophilia quickly spread although research suggests that the concerns were a tad bit exaggerated.

While MySpace popularized hugely in the States, Orkut became popular in Brazil and then gradually gained popularity in India. Mixi achieved wide acceptance in Japan while Lunar Storm achieved recognition in Sweden, Dutch users linked through Hyves, Grono acquired Poland, Hi5 was popular in South America, Europe, Latin America and Bebo expanded their popularity in New Zealand, Australia and United Kingdom.

Facebook began in 2004 in Harvard as an indigenous site. For joining a user needed a harvard.edu email address. As Facebook began introducing it to other schools, the user's pre requisite was to have a valid university email address associated with those schools, a feature that kept the site comparatively personal as to other global SNSs. "Beginning in September 2005, Facebook expanded to include high school students, professionals engaged in the corporate world, and then eventually everyone". The new users could easily get through the profiles of the acquainted users while acquiring access to major corporate sector networks still required the appropriate .com address. The high school users required administer permission to gain access to the Facebook account login. Facebook users are unable to make their full profiles public to all users.

As of now, Facebook and Twitter are the largest social networking sites. Instagram is giving a close fight to these as it is now referred to as the newest SNS of our times. WhatsApp too gave a tight fight to the above SNSs but it has now recently been bought by Facebook. Websites dedicated to interest of various communities are flourishing; SNSs generally revolve around people, not interests. Earlier the various online networks and discussion forums were organized via topics as per topical basis, but today, the social network sites are as personal as it can get involving and focusing on their own communities most importantly. This more precisely demonstrates the distinct social structures, where the world is composed of networks, not groups. SNS have established a new organizational framework for online communities, and along with it, a exciting new research context has started.

Another study was conducted to analyse which SNS was trending among the avid users. Among the largely growing SNS, Facebook seemed to top the list with maximum users. Facebook statistics indicate that its global members have rapidly increased from 150 million to about 350 million between January and December 2009 (Eldon, 2009). "Facebook is used by students to maintain relationships with individuals they are familiar with who live near and far" (Quan-Haase & Young, 2010). "Facebook makes it simpler to communicate with multiple people at one time and to monitor activities of people they have not seen in a while as well as reconnecting with new and old friends" (Quan-Haase & Young, 2010).

"What's up" or "What's happening" are some of the questions that people frequently ask when they are having a conversation or talking on the phone with their close friends. In social media, they present a new opportunity for businesses. Hence, different types of social media networks have emerged. Firstly, there are sites such as YouTube and Facebook where users share images and videos etc. This type of media has obtained popularity by innovating communication techniques which were earlier concentrated on mass communication and its media techniques. In other words, social network is an "open media for interactive communication led by normal people." Social media permit anybody to become an editor, producer and director of any type of content, and deliver it through their own way to their reader's. Social media in the form of a communication based on relationships dissimilar the one-way production and transfer of news, information and entertainment from main media outlets via the mass media.

Social media is set up itself as the alternative of media all across the world and it has leaded to its unpredictable growth within 4-5 years of its birth particularly in the case of western countries, where a wide range of age groups ranging from children to the middle-aged use social media. According to Google's Ad Planner, "15 percent of those aged 17 or below, 9 percent of those aged 18 to 24, 18 percent of those aged 25 to 34, 25 percent of those aged 35 to 44, 19 percent of those aged 45 to 54, and 14 percent of those aged 55 or older are using one form of social media or another".

There are so many reasons that can clarify the rising popularity of social media. Firstly, social media facilitate users to express themselves freely. It's a handy outlet for their aspiration to standout and attracts attention. Social media networks such as Twitter, personal blogs and Facebook are suitable tools to gain appreciation and reveal one. Secondly, people can find out the newest information on anything they want to know. Information is arriving from a "timeline" shown on Facebook has more use to them because it is not from the internet or a newspaper, but from somebody they know. This kind of news from someone they know is more relevant than any kind of haphazard news from the mass media. For example, a suggestion or an outlook on a topic of interest from their friends is more valuable than a stranger's recommendation when making a purchase. Thirdly, people always have a desire to "peep", to see how the people they are involved in are doing. "adding friends" on Facebook , "following" on Twitter , using the RSS feed on a blog, allow users to come across out what other people are doing and what they want to say. Lastly, People can get away from the monotony in their lives. Daily life can be monotonous for most people, which is why a lot of people try to bring change to their lives. Social media helps users to use other people's lives to escape from their own.

Network externalities

Network externalities can be defined as the value or effect that users obtain from a product or service that will bring about more values to consumers with the increase of users, complementary product, or service (Katz and Shapiro, 1985). Hence when the amount of users reaches a critical and a high number, it attracts more people to join in. Many researchers (Gupta & Mela, 2008; Katz & Shapiro, 1985; Lin & Bhattacherjee, 2008) have pointed out the two types of network externalities which are direct and indirect. Direct externalities refer to the increase in the number of users because of an already high number of people using it hence increasing the user's benefit. Many researchers (Gupta & Mela, 2008; Iimi2005; Kim, Park, & Oh, 2008; Pae & Hyun, 2002; Wu, Chen, & Lin, 2007; Yang & Mai, 2010) have claimed that utility for users is derived from market size, impacting the way that people use telecom facilities, computer software, and web-sites. On the other hand, indirect externalities display an increased sense of user value and the benefits arising to the user because the product. It is evaluated by its utility. In addition, a number of researchers (Lin& Bhattacherjee, 2008, 2009) believed that the utility for users also comes from social effects. In the case of instant messaging (e.g., MSN Messenger), the more friends that join the network, the more users can maintain or develop their individual social circles, thereby increasing the utility for users. In the end the main network externalities that were considered to be the main driving force of the generation to join various SNS are direct, Indirect and peer externalities. Hence, these sources of network externalities were mentioned in the study to explore their effects on individual's continued intention to use SNS.

Extent of usage of social media

"Out of the total users of social networks, about 57% are 18-29 years old and have a personal profile on various social media websites" (Lenhart et al, 2010). "The time spent every day by these users varied greatly (Pempek, Yermolayeva, and Calvert, 2009). Most users spent approximately 30 minutes a day on socializing on various sites, mainly through the evening hours 9 P.M. to 12 A.M. Students spent an average of 47 minutes a day on Facebook". "More than 50% of the college students visit a social networking site many times a day (Sheldon, 2008). Quan-Haase and Young (2010) also found that about 82% of college students out of those using social networking sites, reported logging into Facebook multiple times in a day". "Older students use Facebook mainly to remain in touch with friends from high school or from their hometowns whereas, younger students use it more frequently than older students" (Pempek et al., 2009).

With the growing popularity of internet technology, it is rational to be curious about its influence on human face-to-face communication. The quantity and quality of interactions in other kinds of media were not affected by social media sites. Online social interactions are component of the total multimedia social relationship, and not a separate entity on its own. Local social relationships prefer using face-to-face communication rather than using the internet. Long distance relationships are constant with the internet along with the telephone. "Internet interactions are considered high in quality and only moderately lower than telephone calls and face-to-face interactions" (Baym et al., 2004).

"Gender is one of the most significant demographic variables affecting social media usage. Both men and women use social media differently. Men are more likely to have a profile on LinkedIn, whereas women are more likely than men to have a profile on Facebook" (Lenhart et al., 2010). "Women were five times more likely than men to use social networking sites (Tufekci 2008)". Sheldon (2008) found that "overall women are more likely to use social media for passing time, maintaining relationships with family and friends, and entertainment. Men mostly use social media to meet new people. College women were more likely than men to use internet for relational purpose, like connecting with family, romantic partners, and friends." (Baym, Zhang, Kunkel, Ledbetter, & Mei-Chen, 2007). "The educational experience of men and women also affects social media use. Men and women with college experience are more likely to use social networking sites frequently" (Lenhart et al., 2010)

Perceived Communication Skills via Social Networks

Young adults join social networking websites as they have to keep up with their social system. "The primary reason reported was to maintain relationships with existing acquaintances that were a part of their social network" (Sheldon, 2008). "Most users interact on these sites to support their pre-existing relations, as against meeting new people" (Boyd & Ellison, 2007), with some exceptions. Another study recommended that instant messaging and Facebook were used to maintain existing social ties and not to meet new people (Quan-Haase et al, 2010). Other major factors in using social media sites included passing time and entertainment (Sheldon, 2008).

"Social media sites allowed easy access to users to keep in touch with their friends and family in a conveniently and easily" (Quan-Haase et al., 2010). "While students continued to communicate with family and friends by posting their personal information, they spent much of the time only viewing the information posted by others without interacting in any way. A study showed that these lurking activities of looking at photographs or reading other individual's profiles or news feed were performed very often by a majority of respondents." (Pempek et al, 2009). This action of providing social updates and providing entertainment constitutes only one-sided communication.

Different users have different communication needs and social media fulfils these needs. Interactions through the internet facilitate communication by allowing users to keep in touch with friends and family easily, finding about activities of other users, and to learn about social events. "The satisfaction received from this social information made the users feel like they were part of a peer network of knowing what was going on about activities and events." (Quan-Haase et al., 2010).

The major communication benefit of Facebook users was overcoming shyness. "Shyness causes individuals to avoid social, face-to-face conversations altogether, so these individuals have less social support and less communication skills. There is a connection between online social media and friendship quality of shy individuals. Shy individuals could much easily interact with others using social networking media as it provides them with a comfortable environment." (Baker& Oswald, 2010). The

Data point out that people who use Facebook for communication had finer quality friendships. Usage of social media leads to improvement in the quality of relationship of the users. "Using Face book resulted in improved quality of relationships as users felt more comfortable as it was simpler to get to know people better without having face-to-face interactions and users gained support system by spending more time communicating over the computer." (Baker & Oswald, 2010).

The social interaction throughout the social media makes it easier to communicate with everybody by keeping in contact with family and friends on a daily basis more often than non-users. Perceived interaction was reported as being more fulfilling in same sex relations rather than cross sec relations. "Communication relations with friends and family were more satisfying than communication relationships with mere acquaintances." (Baym et al, 2007).

Self-concept and social media

Social media provides a simplified way to communicate with peers and receive feedback from them. Adolescent's attitudes of themselves can be deeply affected by using social media networking sites (Pempek et al., 2009). "Social media sites play an active role in the process of socialization and construction of the self-identity of its users." (Urista et al., 2009). "The users present themselves through a personal profile and can include as much information they want about them including pictures. This self-disclosure is a way of how they want others to perceive them by opening up their own identities." (Pempek et al., 2009). "One way to improve self-concept is by creating an attractive personal profile for others to admire. Computer-mediated communication brings greater intimacy in self-disclosure than in face-to-face contacts." (Jiang, Bazarova, & Hancock, 2011).

"Users participate in selective self-presentation on social media networks to want to impress others." (Jiang et al., 2011). "This is essentially true for college students who self-disclose regularly during this probing period." (Arnett, 2000). "Self-disclosure assists by getting feedback from peers that help strengthen existing relationships and develop a sense of self as well." (Pempek et al., 2009). "Self-disclosure has become an identity challenge in surfacing and emerging adulthood i.e., between 18-25 years of age." (Pempek et al., 2009). It is thought that if an individual has a greater number of friends, "likes" on their pictures, more followers etc on social networking sites, he/she tends to be more admired and hence more popular. A survey concluded that teenagers have an average of 200 people on their Facebook friend list. "Out of which most of them they had met in person before the connection through internet." (West, Lewis, & Currie, 2009). "Additionally, another study found that in order to impress others, young adults created a virtual identity in which they fashioned an ideal self. This procedure of improving self- appearance and capital increased one's self-esteem and self-concept in both the online and the offline world." (Urista et al., 2009).

On average, 80% of Facebook friends were peers of the same age group. Behaviour changed when users were asked about adding other older adults (like parents) as friends on Facebook. Some people said that adding older adults like parents and other family members would invade their personal space and there needs to be a separation in their family life and social life. "This study indicated that being friends with parents on Facebook may lead to problems as it threatens their self-concept because their private has now become public." (West et al., 2009).

"Self-disclosures in social media rely on other people's interpretations on these disclosures and the communication behaviours that follow it." (Jiang et al., 2011). Social media helps to improve the quality of life in college students as they receive social support from other users which helps maintaining existing relationships (Lui & LaRose, 2008). The self-image of individuals improves when they obtain comments from others on pictures and wall posts. It becomes a way of attaining attention from a wide variety of individuals in an indirect way. "A timely response extracts good feelings about self, gratification and fulfillment of personal and interpersonal wants." (Urista et al., 2009). "High disclosure produces relationship intimacy." (Jiang et al., 2011).

Popularity of social media for business

Social media has value for business in four major aspects: time, audiences, cost and relations.

TIME: Speed and durability

In social media networks, information is dispersed promptly (Speed) and has a long-lasting impact (Durability) as compared with mass media. Users can simply communicate through short text messages and post them on micro blogs like twitter (up to 140 characters). Bloggers and YouTube users can broadcast content instantly without having to be concerned with meeting broadcasting schedules or editorial deadlines same as in the case of mass media. Comparatively faster delivery is there in the case of social media than mass media as it is done through the interaction of the users. According to a study, the majority of the social media users transmit the information received within the hour. In the case of social networking site Twitter, 35 percent of its users retransmit content within 10 minutes and 55 percent of them within an hour. Also, the impact of the content remains continuous once it has been released. Social media content is often saved as files and can be uploaded again unlike broadcast news which is exposed and then disappears.

AUDIENCE: Plurality and diversity

The reach of social media is to a more diverse range of users in comparison with mass media.

The kind of connection in social media requires fewer steps for sharing information. The network is formed through voluntary connection and caters to a large number of people creating a "small- world" network. In the case of Twitter, anything tweeted to an average of four people can reach any person in the world. Content is retransmitted to a wider audience when they are introduces to any other form of media. For example, blog content is linked onto Twitter, which is then reported through mass media. Furthermore, social media exceeds both nationality and class. Social media is capable of delivering a message to anyone in the world; word of mouth cannot go so far. Former CEO of Sun Microsystems, Jonathan Schwartz, "continued to communicate with the public through social media and even tweeted his last goodbye, a case in point that the world is entering a new era of World of Mouth (global) from Word of Mouth (local)".

COST: Feasibility and Effectiveness

"Costs can be greatly reduced by using social media as the distribution phase that is needed in mass media, is eliminated. Most of the social media networks are accessed free of cost. For banner ads, 1,000 clicks cost a mere $20." (YouTube, in 2007). There is no need for companies to use celebrities or hire an advertising agency. In addition, issue-by-issue advertising, the expansion of target groups and promotions are possible at a lower cost. YouTube offers free of cost statistical data on access regions, age and gender, time of access, which offers a greater understanding of a range of demographics, consumption patterns and lifestyles. By using this, companies can send out information, targeting different user networks. The Italian luxury fashion brand, Dolce and Gabbana, invited famous bloggers to attend its show and post their opinions on its blog and Twitter page in real-time. "This attracted feedback from tens of thousands of people of fashion world across the globe, resulting in the company enjoying a promotional effect at a much lower cost".

RELATIONS: Friendliness and Credibility

Relationships in social media are recognized on adding each other as friends and through interactions, involving a two-way communication. Hence, genuine communication, trust-building and heart-to-heart are possible. Through honestly sharing daily affairs, companies are able to display their distinct traits and friendly image of their brands. They can also make their brands more familiar by encouraging customer participation in various events on burning issues and in innovative campaigns. Levi's was able to become closer to its customers by launching the "iSpyLevi's" campaign in Australia. Levi's offered clues as to the current location of its agents wearing Levi's jeans on Twitter, and gave the jeans to those who found the agents. Moreover, interactive communication with customers can eradicate misunderstandings which can happen during one-way communications and assist build corporate trust. Interaction also fosters support groups while improving company reputation. If a company has trustworthy supporters, there is prevention of a small problem transpiring into a crisis.

CHAPTER VII

Impact Of Social Media On Life Style

Social Media can be defined as a form(s) of electronic communication through which users create online communities to share information, ideas, personal messages, and other content. It enables the users to see what is happening in different parts of the world by means of the social media accounts of other people rather than through media, news channels and magazines.

Looking back over the last 10-15 years, if we were to think of technology enabled innovations that have had a widespread effect on the whole society, there will be a few contenders. The ease of access to Internet, the advancement in mobile and smart phone technology and the birth of social media will definitely be amongst this list of contenders.

Impact of Social Media on Work Culture & Business

In regards to business, social media can be looked at in two different perspectives, internally and externally. Internally, social media benefits the business in four ways:

- Emotional capital
- Crowd accelerated innovation
- Business continuity planning
- Big data and social media analytics

Emotional Capital is the feeling(s) that employees have towards their employer. If these feeling are good, then the productivity of employees shoots up. With social media, employees can share their ideas and suggestions then get feedback from colleagues, and when the senior managers pick up on this and implement some of the suggestions, the employees are happy, leading to a productivity boost. Also, this allows greater transparency and builds confidence about the company and its leadership. With employees interacting and sharing ideas, problems and getting solutions and feedback from colleagues, crowd accelerated innovation is bound to happen. An example of an internal social networking site is Planet Blue, Intel's internal social networking site. It connects all the employees enabling them to blog, update statuses and wikis. Employees can form groups based on their hobbies. It comes equipped with Intelpedia, a simulation of Wikipedia, open for employees to update their new findings and edit them subsequently.

Social Media Analysis is helping companies to measure social conversations, gain market intelligence, and measure social campaign effectiveness. Externally businesses can also benefit. Social media is a new way for retailers to advertise their new products and services. It provides another medium for marketing and customer interaction. But before a business can start using social media, it needs to state clearly its objectives in terms of investment. It will need to find specific talent for managing its social network use. Different sites are used differently Ex: Twitter is more of a listening site, Facebook is more for customer interaction and Google+ is more integrated with all Google products enabling teamwork and coordination.

But this talent is not easy to come across. Selecting employees who have good skills in these areas and are able to engage with customers can be a challenge. The company will need to educate their employees on how to use social media to obtain the organization's goal. In addition, time will be spent in locating, editing, scheduling and creating content for publishing onto the media. Social media is not risk free either, competitors might try to bash or even hire people to highlight your shortcomings or ruin your reputation. Samsung was fined in Taiwan $340000 recently for doing this with its competitor HTC. Hackers could take over the company accounts and cause severe damage. Malware can be downloaded by employees accessing social sites in the company; therefore companies must have a social media policy. In Ireland 46% of the business do not have a social media policy and 80% of Irish employee access social media at work.

There has been a huge explosion in the social networks over the past 7 years or so. We have a social network for almost every topic – be it games, dating, videos, professional world etc. Among the leaders, Facebook has reached 1.35 billion users all over the world as of 30 October 2014 and Twitter has over 500 million users now. This boom in the social networking world has impacted the way we communicate, interact and socialize in our daily lives. Billions of users interact over the vast range of social networks and discuss about all possible topics. But this makes us prone to the evils of social networking. There is huge amount of data generated on these websites, which makes it difficult for the companies to keep control of.

Being able to connect with peers is a vital piece of the corporate social media value proposition, says Hope Koch, a Baylor University associate professor of information systems. And those connections don't all have to be directly related to a specific project or business outcome. Social media tools can also serve to build a stronger corporate culture by fostering more personal connections, she says.

Koch studied the use of social media at a large financial firm where new recruits built a homegrown network to connect and collaborate. The employees, who had been recruited from college campuses all over the country, used the site to share information about apartments and restaurants, help each other get acclimated to the company, and build new friendships in an unfamiliar environment. "It humanized the workplace," she says.

These softer connections benefited both the employees and the business, because it led to a greater sense of organizational commitment and better employee engagement. "For millennials, mixing their work life and their social life via online social networking created positive emotions for the employees who use the system," Koch says. "These emotions led to more social networking and ultimately helped the employees build personal resources like social capital and organizational learning."

This type of personal engagement drives direct business value, Yates says. Research from Towers Watson shows that highly engaged employees generally produce better business outcomes than their less-engaged co-workers. The research also shows that organizations with high levels of sustainable engagement--which describes the intensity of employees' connection to their organization--enjoyed an average one-year operating margin close to three times higher than that of organizations with low levels of engagement.

GE is already seeing such benefits because of Collab. The platform has more than 200,000 active users, and the response has been overwhelmingly positive. "We solve problems faster, and we have more confidence in the business choices we make,"

Utterbeck says. GE's leadership is equally impressed, giving Utterbeck full support for the project. "They want people from all levels of the organization to be able to collaborate and communicate just as if we were a small company," he says. By harnessing the power of social media, he's enabling just that. (http://www.workforce.com/articles/companies-that-don-t-embrace-social-media-might-be-treading-water-experts-say)

Social Media Increases the Responsibility of Remaining Connected

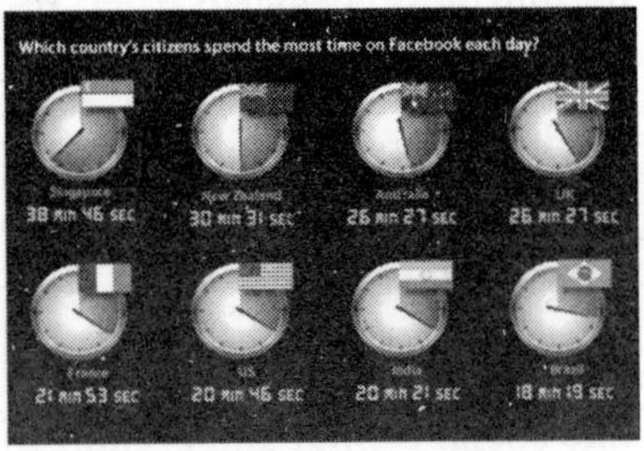

The use of social media as a form of communication has allowed people to be more accessible than ever before. Since communications are quicker, people's expectations of staying connected to each other has also grown multifield. In this situation, where it is so easy to connect with even those people who are miles away, it becomes an obligation to maintain contact and regularly communicate with family, friends, and professional contacts. If not handled properly it may complicate relationships and induce misunderstandings between people

The Impact of social media on Communication

Only 10 years ago, finding and connecting with people that you may have known earlier but lost touch with, was very difficult despite having the power of the Internet& the web. A person would lose touch with people permanently, if they moved away. However, social media sites have completely changed the scenario by making it very easy for people to find each other and reconnect, even after being apart for several years. Social media is a great way to stay in touch with friends, meet new people with similar interests and be part of a community. It also allows you to stay updated with what is happening in the lives of those who are close to you.

Impact of social media on Vocabulary

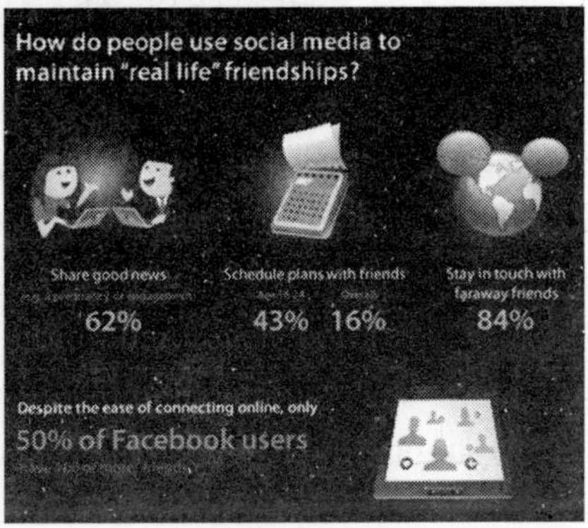

Social media has also had an effect on our language by reinventing the meaning of some words of our vocabulary. For instance, in case of Pinterest, which enables it users to create, mark and share interesting, new ideas through visual bookmarks and introduced a new meaning to the words – pin, pinning and pinned. Originally, we would associate these words with a physical pin that we may use for pinning a paper or a picture to a corkboard, however now in the online world, we often hear people saying – check out my Pin or I was pinning while eating breakfast today. The concept of "pinning" in the online word is similar, just to a board that exists digitally.

Impact of social media on the Youth

For most of our young generation, the use of social media is an integral part of daily life. They find it easier to learn and adapt to new technologies as compared to the older generations. While

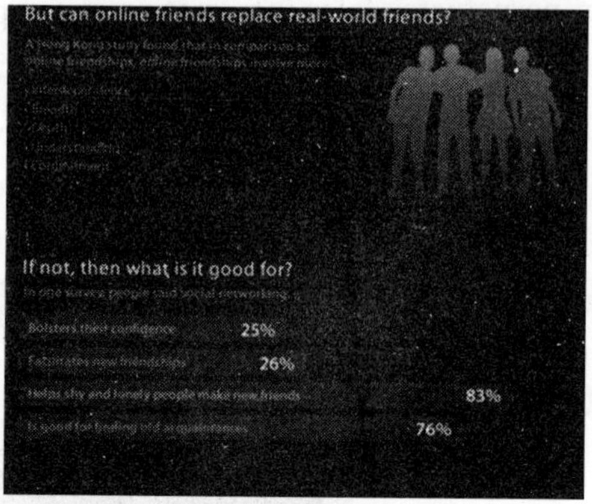

we cannot deny the positive aspects of social media, it also has a negative impact on the social and sexual wellness of the younger generation. If we talk about adolescence, it is a time for self-discovery and transformation. Traditionally, it was your friends, parents and society who would impact the thinking of teenagers and adolescents, but in today's world various social media platforms are playing this critical role. These websites allow social interaction and have enhanced the flow of information and communication worldwide through user's profiles that represents a person's identity. Social Media attracts a lot of young users as they can self-promote themselves in a way they want the world to see them whereas the reality may be different.

In this digital age, popularity is considered by how many comments or likes one get on the content they share online. This promotes people to cross their boundaries on online platforms in order to prove their self-worth. They try to seek attention by taking bolder steps, which can prove dangerous or harmful in their offline life by impacting their self-esteem.

Seeking the validation of others or taking it social media too seriously sometimes results in people being abused by cyber bullies. A Cyber bully is someone who deliberately uses social media

humiliates or perpetuates false information about people. Similar to offline bullying, studies show that online bullying can lead to depression, anxiety, isolation and poor self-esteem.

Impact of social media on Health

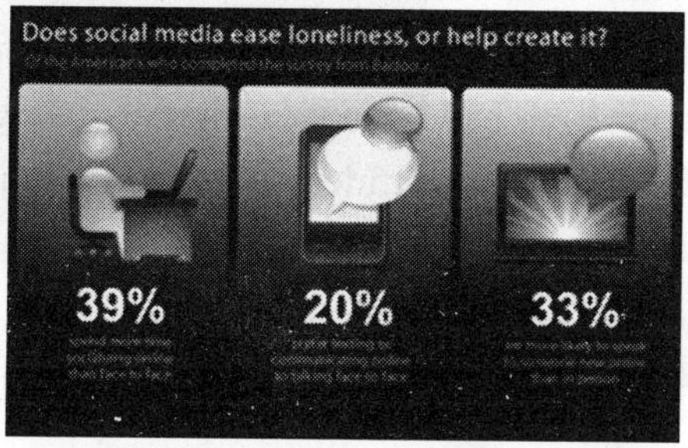

Our lives have become so dependent on social media now that we cannot imagine even one day without logging on to the internet, using our mobile phones and checking our social media accounts. There may be some serious effects on people's health due to excessive use of social media.

- **Addiction:** Research has indicated that people who use social media very regularly tend to get addicted to it. This addiction can cause the individuals to spend enormous amounts of time online; thereby completely changing the way people live their lives.
- **Isolation:** The popularity of social media messages and text messages has made our interactions with people effortless. This in turn has resulted in people isolating themselves, as most of their conversations are online. Social media sites also allow people to hide behind their online identities and live a false life through online channels.
- **Inhibits Physical Interaction with Others:** Online socializing has replaced the traditional forms of socializing and face to face communication. This is leading to the loss of important aspects & human qualities of communication

i.e., basic verbal communication, facial expression, tone of voice and body language.

In 2012, Anxiety UK conducted a survey on social media use and its effects on emotions. The survey found that 53% of participants said social media sites had changed their behaviour, while 51% of these said the change had been negative. Those who said their lives had been worsened by using social media also reported feeling less confident when they compared their achievements against their friends.

Impact of Social Media Marketing

Social media marketing is a form of Internet Marketing that implements various social media networks in order to achieve marketing communication and branding goals. It includes social sharing of content, videos, and images for marketing purposes and its major benefits include, wide reach, advertising through word of mouth, direct connection with customers, brand awareness, increased customer service, low-cost engagement, sales, and it can give a powerful web presence for small companies. However, it has certain disadvantages like it can be very time consuming, negative comments about your brand can go viral in a few seconds. It is something very new so, some companies may not have prior knowledge about it and competitors may copy your marketing strategies as they are all available online.

On an average, companies now use several social media platforms to market their products. The top 7 social media platforms companies like Facebook, Twitter, LinkedIn, Instagram, Google + and YouTube, all use social media marketing for Advertising. Facebook is number one as it has 1.35 monthly users, giving companies a gigantic reach.

The Facebook Culture

On May 18, 2012, when Facebook first issued its stock for IPO, it was followed up by a number of questions on Facebook's social marketing platform and strategy. Surveys conducted by Goldman Sachs and Compete found that social networking sites were the least influential factors in purchasing. Facebook counter surveyed this to demonstrate the fact that being a fan or brand on Facebook leads to more frequent purchases and enhances your popularity. There are various steps that Facebook provides for businesses to be successful. Steps include building a page, connecting with the people by creating an advertisement and engaging your audience. Facebook is also introducing new features like Nearby, Facebook Offer, Graph Search etc. that will help businesses to grow faster. If we talk about advertising on Facebook, it's a three-way process: the business creates an advertisement, Facebook gets paid to show it and the right people see the it. Facebook decides which advertisements are relevant to us by monitoring our activities such as status updates, page likes, groceries we buy or the game we play. Currently, 88% of US companies use Facebook for marketing purposes.

We looked at some Facebook campaigns that have been successful in the past.

Corona Light: In 2010, Corona Light aimed to become the "most liked light beer in America." With its Facebook app customers were invited to put their face in Times Square, NYC. It got thousands of people to "like" Corona Light's Facebook page, where the company could deliver even more marketing messages and news about its beers.

Jack in the box: In October 2010, popular American fast food chain Jack in the Box added 5c to a prize pool for each person that "liked" the company's page on Facebook. One man was chosen at random out of 283,000 fans and won the pool after 3 weeks of the campaign. During the contest, Jack in the Box's Facebook page saw a 280% increase in fans.

Bing and Farmville: In March 2010, Microsoft gained over 400,000 Facebook fans on their Bing fan page thanks to a single advertisement in FarmVille. The fan page, which grew by five times in size was part of a promotion by Bing, where Farmville users could gain virtual currency by becoming a fan of the Bing Facebook page. By clicking on a sponsored ad on the bottom right of the FarmVille main page, they'd receive 3 Farm Cash.

When it comes to Facebook, ads are displayed even if users are not searching for anything. On the other hand, ads in Google are shown as part of the search result.

If Facebook can find out a way to draw a correlation between likes and sales and how companies make profit from Facebook's social marketing.

Twitter's Increasing Popularity

In 2012, social networking sites continued to surprise all of us. Twitter is like all other social networking sites such as Facebook, YouTube, Pinterest, Flicker etc. as it provides the users with a platform to express themselves, by creating & sharing content with others called "followers"- who sign up to receive someone's "tweets". The main assets of Twitter are User Attention, Audience Size (eyeballs per day), Database of tweets, Alternative Media Platform and its Unique Selling Propositions lies with the fact that it is Spontaneous and "Real Time" observations.

Twitter has accomplished enormously financially, and it has managed to attract a large amount of users since it was created in 2006. By 2012, Twitter had an estimated 500 million registered users worldwide and the first half of this year saw them making revenue of $254 million. As per the stats for 2012, Twitter generated approximately 64 cents per user in the last 3 months (Meanwhile in the same period LinkedIn made $1.53 and Facebook made $1.58 per user). Twitter monetizes on these assets through: Advertising, Temporal Real time search and E-Commerce Sales platform. In 2009 Pear Analytics analysed the Content of the Tweets, which measures the relevance of Tweet content for the year 2009.

Twitter is a powerful alternative media platform for the distribution of news, videos and pictures, but who would have thought that Twitter would be at the forefront in reporting the terrorist attacks in Mumbai, the Iranian rebellion in 2009, the political violence in Bangkok and Kenya in May 2010 and the uprisings in Egypt, Tunisia and other areas in the middle East and Africa in 2011.

The future of a publicly traded Twitter is big. Twitter has acquired ad serving platform, MoPub, which means reduced advertisements on your stream. Twitter is coming up with interest graphs based on who you follow and words you tweet about. Selling these interest graphs through MoPub platform would be a new source of revenue for Twitter. Advertising partnerships with TV networks is also a focus for Twitter going forward. . Twitter is exploring the possibility of allowing TV networks to stream live clips of video to users who have seen, or may be interested in their content. Most shows, and even some ads, show a hash tag in the bottom corner of the screen to encourage fans to tweet while viewing. Another speculation is that Twitter could offer a paid subscription option for users to not see promoted content. Let's say just 2 million people, 1% of Twitter's 200 million users, paid for such a service of $3; these subscription-based members would generate $6 million cash/month for the company.

CHAPTER VIII

Social Networking And Its Addiction

As we have read social networking sites as predominantly used for creating profiles on the internet and establishing connectivity with the various users who have done the same. This, however, does not end there. Anything done in inadequate amount is harmful and so is social networking. Addiction to social networking sites is considered a mental and health problem. As per a famous psychologist, escapism, ignorance of oneself, pre occupation of mind and intolerance are the various symptoms seen in a SNS addictive being.

There are five major types of internet addiction, namely "computer addiction (i.e., computer game addiction), information overload (i.e., web surfing addiction), net compulsions (i.e., online gambling or online shopping addiction), cyber sexual addiction (i.e., online pornography or online sex addiction), and cyber-relationship addiction (i.e., an addiction to online relationships)". Social networking addiction seems to fall in the 'cyber relationship' addiction category since the main idea behind the active use of social media is establishing connections.

Social media addiction can be related to any substance related addiction as it follows the same manner of addiction, shows the same symptoms and is offered the same cure. The potential detrimental consequences of both the addictions are also rather same.

Social networking is now a global phenomenon. Majority people surfing the internet utilize their time on social networking sites. The addiction initially seemed to show more in boys than girls as girls used the SNSs to maintain contact rather than forming new contact. More than ½ the teenagers started using social media actively by visiting their profiles at least thus increasing the time spent on the SNSs by 2 hours each day and thus a total of 30% increase in online activity participation from '09 to '10.

In addition, it was also brought to notice that teenagers and young adults use the social media more in relation to the adults as they are aware of the constant changes and thus maintain and update their profile regularly. Thus, constant use of such activities may stimulate the neurological pathways that thus show addiction and indulgence in the social media.

Reasons And Consequences for Addiction to Social Media

1. The addiction problem starts when one spends majority time on various sites like Facebook, twitter, Instagram while browsing the net. The problem arises when not one day passes without opening such sites and updating your profile.
2. Once the indulgence in the social network is started, everything else escalates quickly. The inflow and outflow of messages, photos and updates is constant and never ending and hence requires regular check in.
3. Social network is also used as a tool of recreation. When one is feeling low and not up to the mark, the indulgence in social networking helps to feel better and thus is a start to SNS addiction.

4. It is also a site used for casual encounters with friends and sometimes strangers but if these sites start taking more time out of your routine and sleep pattern then these sites have started causing you trouble.

Steps to Gradually Eradicate The Addiciton

1. Recognizing, identifying and accepting that one has a problem. Acceptance is the first step to cure. Once one is aware of one's problem, they are more likely to remove it from their systems.
2. If one has an urge to open and update their SNS account, they must step back and realize that they joined to maintain contact with their loved ones and not lose touch of their families and friends thy live with.
3. Prepare a time table with time slots for recreational activities and considering SNS indulgence as one of those activities.
4. Following the time table that one made and promising one to only use these sites when one's work for the day is over.
5. Remove those people from the list whose updates are not of much importance in your life. This will help you to spend less time on the sites as only information about the valuables will be shown.
6. If one cannot control oneself then they should install and application called 'Cold Turkey' which prevents you from log in to addictive sites.
7. If everything else fails and there is no sign of self-control, one can always resolve to deactivation of one's account. Remember, it's for your own good.

CHAPTER IX

Social Media Ethics

While scholarship in the social and natural sciences has tended to focus on the impact of SNS on psychological markers of happiness/well-being, psychological adjustment, social capital or feelings of life satisfaction, philosophical concerns about social networking and ethics have generally cantered on topics amenable to empirical measurement (e.g.: privacy, identity, friendship, the good life and democratic freedom). More so than social capital or feelings of life satisfaction these topics are closely tied to traditional concerns of ethical theory (e.g.: virtues, rights, duties, motivations and consequences). These topics are also tightly linked to the novel features and distinctive functionalities of SNS, more so than some other issues of interest in computer and information ethics that relate to more general internet functionalities, e.g., issues of copyright and intellectual property.

1. Social networks and privacy

Social networking technologies have added a new sense of urgency and new layers of complexity to the existing debates among philosophers about computers and informational privacy. The issue of privacy is one pivotal to the lives of individuals. It is the most impactful of all. A lot of cybercrimes have cantered on this and almost everything revolves on it.

We will discuss why privacy and ethics related to it are so important. Some fundamental practices of concern include: the potential availability of users' data to third parties for commercial, surveillance or data mining purposes; the capacity of facial recognition software to automatically identify persons in uploaded photos; the ability of third-party applications to collect and publish users' data without their permission or awareness; the frequent use by SNS of automatic, 'opt-in' privacy controls; the use of 'cookies' to track online users activities after they have left a SNS; the potential use of location-based social networking for stalking or other illicit monitoring of users' physical movements; the sharing of user information or patterns of activity with government entities; and, last but not least, the potential of SNS to encourage users to adopt voluntary but imprudent, ill-informed or unethical information sharing practices, either with respect to sharing their own personal data or sharing data related to other persons and entities. Facebook has been a particular lightning-rod for criticism of its privacy practices. But it is just the most visible member of a far broader and more complex network of SNS actors with access to unprecedented quantities of sensitive personal data.

These new actors in the information environment create particular problems with respect to privacy norms. For e.g., since it is the ability to access information freely shared by others that makes SNS uniquely attractive and useful, and given that users often minimize or fail to fully understand the implications of sharing information on SNS, we may find that contrary to traditional views of information privacy, giving users greater control over their information-sharing practices may actually lead to decreased privacy for themselves or others. Moreover, in the shift from (early web 2.0) user-created and maintained sites and networks to (late web2.0) proprietary social networks, many users have yet to fully process the potential for conflict between their personal motivations for using SNS and the profit-driven motivations of the corporations that possesses the data.

Scholars also note the way in which SNS architectures are often insensitive to the granularity of human sociality. That is, such architectures tend to treat human relations as if they are all of a kind, ignoring the profound differences among types of social relations (familial, professional, collegial, commercial, civic etc.)

As a consequence, the privacy controls of such architectures often fail to account for the variability of privacy norms within different but overlapping social spheres. Contextual integrity demands that our information practices respect context-sensitive privacy norms, where 'context' refers not to the overly coarse distinction between 'private' and 'public', but to a far richer array of social settings characterized by distinctive roles, norms and values.

On the design side, such complexity means that attempts to produce more 'user-friendly' privacy controls face an uplift challenge- they must balance the need for simplicity and ease of use with the need to better represent the rich and complex structures of our social universe. A key design question, then, is how SNS privacy interfaces can be made more accessible and more socially intuitive for users.

Finally, privacy issues with SNS highlight a broader philosophical problem involving the intercultural dimensions of information ethics; Rafael Capurro has noted the way in which narrowly Western conceptions of privacy occlude other legitimate ethical concerns regarding new media practices. For example, he notes that in addition to western worries about protecting the private domain from public exposure, we must also take care to protect the public sphere from the excessive intrusion of the private. Though he illustrates the point with a comment about intrusive uses of cell phones in public spaces, the rise of mobile social networking has amplified this concern by several factors. When one must compete with Facebook or twitter for the attention of not only one's dinner companions and family members, but also one's fellow drivers, pedestrians, students, movie-goers, patients, and audience members, the integrity of the public sphere comes to look as fragile as that of the private.

2. The Ethics of Identity and Community on Social Networking Services

Technologies social networking open up a new type of ethical space in which personal identities and communities, both 'real' and virtual, are constructed, presented, negotiated, managed and performed. SNS such as Facebook can also be viewed as enabling authenticity in important ways. While the 'Timeline' feature displaying my entire online personal history can prompt me to' edit' my past, it can also prompt me to face up to and assimilate into my thoughts and actions that might otherwise be conveniently forgotten. Also, there can be multiple identities of a single user which maybe authentic according to the standards of a social networking sites, but may not be authentic in reality. This duality or dichotomy related to identities creates a dangerous situation for people.

3. Friendship, Virtue and The Good Life on Social Networking Services

SNS can facilitate many types of relational connections: LinkedIn encourages social relations organized around our professional lives, Twitter is useful for creating lines of communication between ordinary individuals and figures of public interest, MySpace was for a time a popular way for musicians to promote themselves and communicate with their fans, and Facebook, which began as a way to link university cohorts and now connects people across the globe, has

Recently seen a surge in business profiles aimed at establishing links to existing and future customers. These sorts of questions about how online friendships measure up to offline ones, along with questions about whether or to what extent online friendships encroach upon users' commitments to embodied, 'real-world' relations with friends, family members and communities, defined the ethical problem-space of online friendship as SNS began to emerge.

4. Democracy, Freedom and Social Networking Services in The Public Sphere

As is the case with privacy, identity, community and friendship on SNS, ethical debates on the impact of SNS on civil discourse, freedom and democracy in the public sphere must be seen as extensions of a broader discussion about the political implications of the Internet. Related topic of concern is the potential of the Internet to fragment the public sphere by encouraging the formation of a plurality of 'echo chambers,' informational silos for like-minded individuals who deliberately shield themselves from exposure to alternative views. The worry is that such insularity will promote extremism and the reinforcement of ill-founded opinions, while also preventing citizens of a democracy from recognizing their shared interests and experiences. Finally, there is the question of the extent to which SNS can facilitate political activism, civil disobedience and popular revolutions resulting in the overthrow of authoritarian regimes.

5. Social Networking Services and Cybercrime

SNS have been targeted, especially in mass media, as potential hosts for a broad spectrum of 'cybercrimes,' including but not limited to: cyber bullying, cyber stalking, child exploitation, illegal surveillance, identity theft, intellectual property and copyright violations. Cybercrime is an enduring topic of philosophical interest for the broader field of computer ethics, and the migration to and evolution of such crime on SNS platforms may raise new and distinctive ethical issues in the coming decades.

6. Social Networking Services and Metaethical Issues

A host of meta-ethical questions are raised by the rapid emergence of SNS as a dominant medium of interpersonal connection. SNS and other emerging information technologies do not reliably confine themselves to national or cultural boundaries, and this creates a particular challenge for applied ethicists. For example, SNS practices in different countries must be analyzed against a conceptual background that recognizes and accommodates complex differences in moral norms and practices concerning, for example, privacy. Other SNS phenomena that one might expect to benefit from intercultural analysis and that are relevant to the ethical considerations include: varied cultural patterns and preference/tolerance for affective display, argument and debate, personal exposure, expressions of political, interfamilial or cultural criticism, religious expression and sharing of intellectual property. Alternatively, the very possibility of a coherent information ethics may juxtapose challenge, for example, from a constructivist view that emerging socio-technological practices like SNS continually redefine ethical norms—such that our analyses of SNS and related technologies are not only ceased to operate from shifting ground, but from ground that is being shifted by the intended object of our ethical judgment. There are, thus, pressing practical concerns about whether and how philosophers can actually have an impact on the ethical profile of emerging technologies such as SNS. If philosophers direct their ethical analyses only to other philosophers, then it is likely such analyses will function simply as ethical postmortems of human-technology relations, with no opportunity to actually pre-empt, reform or redirect unethical technological practices.

Ethics in Using Facebook

The popularity of Facebook is growing immensely in all walks of life. With the growing usage of social Networking, it is very important for one to know where to draw the line. To avert an ethical crisis there is an urgent need to understand the importance of moral use of Facebook. The best practices for using Facebook must be developed. With these new opportunities come new responsibilities and hence social responsibility must be given priority while accessing the net. This section analyses such significant factors. With such social communication being made and transmitted digitally, researchers from fields in the sciences and both physical and social sciences have exploited this rich source of data. Facebook by its nature comprises joints between millions of users, and many concerns arise because of this.

Interaction is the lifeblood of human existence. It helps us to build relationships with others and with the world. Ethics guide us how we should act or behave in a particular position like professional, family etc. these ethics are guidelines are to be copied and applied while interacting with the virtual world specially Facebook.

Social networking sites like Facebook have created a web of easy connectivity. Social networking sites are the most important part of human life in the modern era; they have become a part and parcel of the common man's life. It facilitates communication at a click of a mouse, business enterprises use social networking sites such as Facebook as a platform for advertising and marketing for Facebook offers a wide reach, with features such as 'news feed' one can also see their 'friends' movements. Facebook also helps in building an educational relationship between students and teachers (Mazman, S. G. & Usluel, Y. K. (2010)). Facebook is a place where you can chat with others, comment on people's status, and add your own status, view friends' photos, 'like' them and much more. With such benefits that Facebook offers, comes great responsibility, and hence the problem of ethical use of Facebook arises. Malpractices such as cyber bullying, hacking, stalking have become really common.

"Facebook is a source of one's personal information which can be misused; such information becomes food for cyber criminals. Social networking sites such as Facebook encourages more and more people to become public about their lives and share their personal information online. One must remember that the internet never forgets. Although Facebook provides its users with many options to keep strangers from viewing their personal details, lack of privacy is major drawback of such sites. Many researchers have mainly emphasized on privacy concerns relating to young users (George, 2006; Kornblum & Marklein, 2006). Once a person has access to someone's personal information, he might misuse it to socially endanger that person. Facebook by default has the settings to make the information available to the largest user base, making it difficult for new users. When the users of the social networking sites give personally identifiable information (PII), like address and date of birth only for benefits to their friends, these users believe that their friends are already aware about their PII and providing this information only provides clarity to their circle of friends." (Comer, R., McKelvey, N., & Curran, K. (2012).

In many cases, the user is unaware of the extent to which their own personal information has spread. One main reason for this kind of confusion is the way social networks enable the settings for the account. Criminals may use personal information provided like a person's location, birthday, hobbies, Interest and routine to imitate a trusted friend or convince the unsuspicious that they have the suitable authority to access financial or personal data. Criminals also might use this information to guess someone's account passwords, because of which one should never have an identifiable password like the name of one's pet, hobby, favourite band, birthday etcetera which is easily known about someone through their social networking sites. It would be of much help to the stalkers if one keeps posting about their daily routines and whereabouts online (www.usatoday.com).

Cyber bullying, another form of unethical computer use. It is getting increasing coverage in the media as it becomes a larger problem. Sitting in front of a computer screen takes away the need to bully and harass someone in person and thus makes even worse actions and humiliation possible. The devastations of these online attacks can leave deeps mental scars; kids especially are prone to such acts (Campbell, M.A (2005)). Social media provides a platform to people to render hateful comments and even threats. The emotional and psychological impacts of cyber bullying are quite similar to those in the case of real-life bullying. The only difference being, real-life bullying often ends when school ends. For cyber bullying, there is no means of escape. Cyber bullying poses many challenges for teachers and educators. Since many still don't have proper knowledge regarding social media, it becomes a task for authorities to handle cyber bullying (Davis, M. R. (2011)).

Fake identities are yet another form of unethical use of Facebook. People can pose as whoever they want and can talk to anyone they want. This can be dangerous, especially for people who post a lot of their personal information online. Such acts facilitate serious crimes such as rapes, human trafficking etc. Film stars, celebrities, politicians face the problem of people pretending to be them and posting things they would not want to.

Facebook has become a distraction for everyone, there is always a reason to log on, to check new status updates, too see new photos, to view endless funny pictures, to play online games or simply, just to kill boredom. People waste a lot of time on Facebook which leads to abnormal sleeping cycles, unhealthy routines and eating habits. Teenagers form the maximum number of people who use Facebook and most of them are constantly logged on either through their phones or computers, the only time they are not using Facebook is when they are asleep. Facebook culture has really had an impact on the young generation, and it is very painful to say that it is becoming a waste of time (Orita, A. & Hada, H. (2009)). One of the major problems that arise with the use of social media is spamming. Spamming is the act of sending unsought for emails to a person who didn't ask for it. Such emails are mostly commercial in nature and mainly comprise of advertisements, promoting useless products. It is important to 'block' such spammers so as to prevent any sort of -interaction with them. Such spammers can prove to be a hindrance to the use of social media as they may discourage new users to join (www.helpaweber.com, www.google.com).

Most importantly, social networking sites such as Facebook addictive. Ironically when many are concerned regarding the privacy issues in using social media, there are many people who willingly share their personal details on sites, this has a lot to do with the social acceptance from their 'friends' that everyone seeks (Song, I., Larose, R., Eastin, M. S., & Lin, C. A. (2004)). Sharing to a certain extent may not prove to be detrimental but the idea of over sharing may create problems. As people might say and share things which they regret later on. Such shared information and details become the fodder for cyber criminals. A social media addict has the habit of checking his or her accounts for updates during free time. This leads to inefficiency as one is distracted and it may be hard to concentrate. The spread of 3G and Wi-Fi networks facilitate this addiction as it acts as a fuel for one to constantly check for updates and responses to their posts. Some people spend a lot of their waking hours in managing their 'friends" impression of them. The problem arises when people start to think too much and try too hard to portray a social image of themselves, especially students (Peluchette, J., & Karl, K., 2009). Ironically when many are concerned regarding the privacy issues in using social media, there are many people who willingly share their personal details on sites, this has a lot to do with the social acceptance from their 'friends' that everyone seeks. Sharing to a certain extent may not prove to be detrimental but the idea of over sharing is the one that should be checked. As people might say and share things which they regret later on. Such shared information and details become the fodder for cyber criminals. A social media addict has the habit of checking his or her accounts for updates during free time. This leads to inefficiency as one is distracted and it may be hard to concentrate. The spread of 3G and Wi-Fi networks facilitate this addiction as it acts as a fuel for one to constantly check for updates and responses to their posts. Some people spend a lot of their waking hours in managing their 'friends" impression of them. The problem arises when people try too hard to portray a social image of them. Some people, just to curb the anxiety of posting something start posting mundane things about their daily routines; this may be classified as obsession. As one gets used to communicating just by a click through social media via, messaging, sharing photos, posts etcetera, people might start finding comfort in socializing online that offline. This is rather unhealthy as face-to-face communication is a far richer experience. One cannot simply hear the tone or notice the body language while talking online; it is very common for text messages to be interpreted in an undesired way, resulting in resentment among chatters.

With the advent of social media many business enterprises have started using social networking sites as a platform for business marketing. Such use also gave rise to malpractices i.e., unethical use of social media (Qualman, E., 2012). One such example is counter-selling one's products. The most common example is to present own product in a superior way than the competitors. This is a classic example of bad marketing manners and it isn't going to win you any friends in your industry. Another such example is Fake Plugs, marketers and business enterprises have their employees pose as a consumer who is a satisfied user of their products and may leave fake comments and reviews about the product. This misleads the actual consumer posting fake comments and bogus reviews is highly unethical and if truth is discovered it will have a major impact on the credibility of the business enterprise. Another unethical use involves building fake profiles and leaving negative reviews and comments about a competitor's product. Social media can also be used as a platform to post bogus industry information and statistics to persuade the consumer to buy a product. (www.reputation.com).

CHAPTER -X

Role Of Social Media In Nation Building

Nation Building is a very vast term, surrounded by historical experiences. It is a process of defining and developing the national identity of a state meaning to develop regional or group identity within the state. Nation building also comprises of constructing roads, airports, electricity lines, raising institutions and organizations, and providing education and services. In order to build confidence in masses, Nation building is very important.

Some leading cases

Nirbhaya

Through Facebook and twitter, users vented their outrage and forced the government to take an action immediately against the accused. There were at least 10 groups created to bring the people together for the cause and it helped since Facebook has the 2nd largest user base in India. People received the reactions through tweets of prominent people who are respected and hold a special place in the society.

With the whole nation connected through social media people were out on the roads protesting and leaving no choice for the government but to address the issue in the right perspective.

AAP's success

Social media has been an important factor in AAP party's success. A party with no political backing and limited resources made its presence felt by connecting through social media like Facebook, twitter, posting videos on YouTube and gathering people to assemble in support by attending rallies.

Revolutions on Facebook

A 29-year-old angered Google marketing executive in Dubai went online and created a Facebook page voicing his concern against the atrocities of the Egyptian Police. Two minutes after he started this page, 300 people had joined it and three months later, it was more than 250000. He gathered opinion polls on the issue raised through the page. He also asked for ideas on how to express through a rally. All the efforts made by this 29 year old inspired the young activist, which initiated the Egyptian Revolution for Democracy in 2011.

Tunisian Revolution

Mohamed bouazizi, a 26-year-old graduate could not get a job. So, he started his own venture of selling vegetables. On being ill-treated by a policeman, he set himself to fire publically in front of the government authorities. The social media was first stopped by the phishing method; there were also Internet and power cuts. Social media activists were also arrested. Dhafer Salhi, the lawyer used social media for organizing the protests through Facebook by sending out invites to friends

Social networking by Indian Government Agencies

Planning commission

This year the planning commission posted its 12th five-year plan on Facebook and this discussion was open for everyone and people could share their thoughts and opinions by giving comments and even status updates and likes. The main motive behind this was to take policy matters to the masses. It builds national integrity and everyone gets a chance to take part in the decision-making by giving ideas and remarks. The current likes on the Facebook page are more than 5000 which have resulted in distinct and remarkable suggestions for the commission which were open for discussion. For polls and publicity, the commission also plans to use twitter.

Delhi Traffic Police

This initiative of social networking bandwagon has already resulted in booking of more than 22,000 offenders, which even include more than 723 policemen and numerous VIPs. This two-way communication channel has been a hit bypassing all the bureaucratic bottlenecks. This page has more than 1.23 lakh members. This is perfect mixture of IT with traffic rules as the users upload the date, time, and location of the offence so no one can be left unprosecuted. Around 18,297 offenders had been prosecuted by 2011 and 3,893 were booked by 30 June by issuing challan for wrong parking, number plates, tinted glass and riding scooters without helmets.

Due to evidence against offenders like MLA, SHO, municipal councilor and their relatives, they were forced to be booked. Some have also misused this by deliberately uploading the wrong details, but these cases have been rear as compared to others. The

Police have been active on the page by giving updates, advisories, traffic scenarios making commuting time faster and better. Even users are posting updates and glitches.

Ministry of External Affairs

It has been more than 3 years now and this page has more than 137k likes. The numbers are also making progress on twitter. The MEA has also presented its blog and has started uploading videos, lectures on YouTube. The MEA will integrate on all of these social networking platforms and offer e-publishing and webcasts.

Indian Railways

For providing instant train status, the railways have opened a page for providing this information. This is currently for Delhi only informing the capital about train platforms, arrival and departure time and journey schedules and the availability of seats on short notice.

It has also included the procedures for those who are unclear about them and reducing the touts as information would be easily available. There is an application, which has been developed for all mobile operating systems.

From this app you can book tickets and download the reservation charts 3 hours before. It is providing up-to- minute information and is linked with National Train Inquiry Service, increasing convenience for the travellers.

Ministry of road transport and highway authority of India have now undertaken a new way, i.e. you can upload a picture of the roads which need repairing which would be addressed by the ministry. All this can be done on their Facebook page. The Reserve Bank of India using its twitter to provide the information about policies, derecognizing a bank etc on social media

Use of social media in the corporate world

In today's corporate world social media is proving to be of immense importance. Now the traditional form of interaction has been obsolete and people who were previously unapproachable can be reached using social media. It has changed the entire hierarchical system. It helps unemployed professionals to look for the possible recruiter, therefore increasing the job opportunities for them. You can connect with the HR staff ask for the job descriptions and inquire about the opportunities. It has enabled to connect the right person for the right job. Job aspirants scan the review for that job Feedback system is being used by the organization in which they are working. Its helps in directly contacting the person who is responsible for the recruitment and who could land you a job. You can connect with carious alumni and highly respected people who can guide you on your career and provide important information about the industry.

It also helps you to keep In touch with your employees, former peers, bosses and colleagues. You can even track their moments and broaden your network. It is help to employers by providing them with the background checks to ensure that your profile portrays you and you are a potential candidate. Additionally, etiquettes should not be forgotten while interacting with the professionals. You should be formal and should not hound the employer with repeated e-mails.

How social media is being used in education.

Being so vast, social media is just a click away and with Google you can find anything, which leads to a faster way of learning. Many types of tools are being used effectively from the last 5-10 years. Some of the tools are

Blogs

They are great for sharing personal information. Good blogs are one of the most efficient learning techniques. It is basically used as a tool to express his information; managing discussions and self-directed learning by access to teachers posted links and themes.

Google+

This connects Students to their teachers by their circle forming s virtual communication. They may need insights on a particular lesson so it acts as a tool to fasten up their learning and make it more effective.

Youtube

It is one of the leaders in online video. It has several categories from the university departments, business enterprises plus a wide range of videos from the masses. It provides a platform for easily distributing the videos with a low budget.

Skype

It is used for setting up virtual meetings by contacting their teachers. Skype has made a portal which is used by educators for conducting lessons. This can be used at any place and at any time. It has been also used for private tutoring.

Twitter

This is used for reminding students about the lectures and the dues assignment dates or the upcoming examinations. Teachers may also use this for sharing their opinions, views or inspirational quotes.

Instagram

Instagram has been really famous among kids so teachers use it as an advantage by using this to upload assignments such as essays. They can even create campaigns for a lesson or an organization

TedED

This offers various talks on various subjects. It is now shaping the new education world by a new approach and ideas on subjects such as health psychology business language etc. It further spreads through social networking by organizing its talk events and further uploading them.

Podcasting

Free creation of classrooms by MP3 and podcasts where students get to view and watch lectures.

Social media as a Tool of Language Learning

By using social media, learning has become interesting, effective and more interactive. Studying has become more enjoyable from this by learning from the native people around the world. This has transformed the traditional classroom teaching with High tech education software and online tools. It has influenced development of languages

One of the most famous website used for learning languages is LIVEMOCHA. It has more than 6 million users building their own profile and indicating the languages they want to learn online by earning points. People use the points to learn a language by correcting/ teaching the language which they are good at and by using those points to learn a newer language

There are several other sites as well and the motive behind this sites is to spread language education through social media.

Social media in Health care

Social media clearly offers a number of health benefits like creating awareness of health issues both preventive and curative.

Facilitating social interaction

SNS help in strengthening existing relationships and encouraging by developing new ones. Research shows that people who are in isolation are more exposed to chronic diseases or disabilities. Social isolation leads to variety of physical and mental problems. By using social media they developed a shared language, which gave people a feeling of belonging.

Building communities

They connect people of same interest, which encourages a feeling of belonging, and acceptance, which helps the users to cope up with their current stressful situation. On these communities people generally share advice and load to the people who are going through this situation or have been through this situation.

More help seeking

Overcoming of the traditional barriers, the youth is now taking all its queries to the Internet for health advices. They are now looking information about sexual or mental health by using chartrooms, watching videos and downloading podcasts. People also anonymously connect to share their experiences which builds the youths confidence

Healthier lifestyle

People are now using social media to achieve goals by sharing their progress by posting regular updates. By sharing they get encouragement as well as feedback so they can be focused on their goal and create a healthy lifestyle. Goals can be to quit smoking, controlling Blood pressure, exercising regularly. They also use social media for campaigning or to promote a cause, which is not beneficial for their health.

How social media is being used to promote tourism

Tourism being the one the most important pillar in the country's economy can be promoted using social media. This platform is giving impressive results if appropriate type of social media is used for promotion. Ie vegas is using twitter list Japan has Facebook pages for all information. New Zealand has created a YouTube channel. A recent trend of tourist checking in has boosted the popularity Foursquare is very common for these Mobile applications are made which helps the tourist to guide themselves throughout the city.

Role of social media in case of natural calamities

Use of online information helps to know what's happening. Mobiles need two-way communication whereas radios are a universal source. But now due to increasing use of smartphones people use tools such as twitter to get location-based information. Social media users forward information. Information related to calamities is one of the most forwarded; users forward this information to ensure that it reaches a wide audience due to which many people are removed from the situation.

Help in monitoring

The victims are taken out from the comfort zone. By monitoring it helps to find out issues which would not been possible to found out using offline means.

Helps in aiding

Red crossed collected 2.5 mil post for review by posting 10,000 photos per second. People can donate to red cross through SNS sites such as Facebook

Social moorings, national perspectives

Given that the social networking phenomenon has unleashed such a massive transformation in global connectivity it is apt and opportune to explore what else can be done with the enormous "social energy" that is created. No doubt, this phenomenon has led to the individual participants discover more meaning in their lives and the business participants achieve greater reach in the social base. At the same time, like the energy of the mighty oceans, the energy of the formidable social networks is often idled, if not wasted, through non-value adding activities. Social scientists even hold that these have become obsessive diversions from other productive activities while some medical specialists hold that the Internet addiction to be a clinical disorder. That said, neither the march of technology nor progress of connectivity can be undone; rather creative ways must be found to channel the enormous social energy on the Internet that is the order of the day. One very relevant channel to direct the social energy would be national missions initially, followed up with global visions. As some of the recent social campaigns have shown, the young and the intelligent have a huge stake in how societies, economies and nations would shape up. This requirement can only be more profound in India than in any nation given that India would have the youngest and largest demographic profile globally for the next several decades. The vision of India racing to be the third largest global economic power by 2035 is tempered by the multitudes of social, economic and industrial inequities and constraints that India has to grapple with.

Contribution to National missions

Social networking communities can contribute to several national missions like enhancing online education, including support systems for parents and educational institutions, especially at primary and secondary levels providing market and technology outreach for micro and small enterprises to promote self-reliance and entrepreneurship, development of national policy initiatives and programs based on community experiences, open source collaboration for up gradation of industrial products and business services, cultural transformation to attain the highest levels of national comparative advantage in terms of innovation, quality and productivity, making India an equitable, safe, ecologically conscious welfare state, women empowerment in all walks of life and enabling them to assume leadership roles in the business and industry, agrarian uplift, enabling the indigent farmer, manage a positive rural economy is the eight mission. Geriatric care with healthcare taken up by voluntary and government contributions is very much a need of the hour. And finally, balanced child nutrition, including, free food for all indigent day care babies and school going children would boost the nation's health and literacy levels even further.

These national missions may seem overwhelming but can be tackled by mass voluntary drive of the educated and employed population, which characterizes the core of the social networking movement. This requires a paradigm shift in the approach to, and use of, social networking. Expansion of the network to create greater levels of social energy and focused channeling of the social energy to national missions would require behavioural underpinnings. There is a need to absorb the Mission. The socially conscious and nationally driven social citizens of the Net should give wide exposure to national missions. The Times Group of India launched a Teach India awareness and voluntary participation campaign to a considerable degree of success. Collaborating with the social networking sites for additional infrastructure and visibility support can help the social netizens see and absorb the national missions.

The national missions can be fulfilled only by a passion to contribute to national upliftment. This requires that the networked citizens understand and analyse their own competencies and capabilities and are fired by a passion to share these with the needy country men and women. Such passion should be shared by the discrete communities so that the ability to contribute is reinforced.

Visibility and passion need to be supplemented with innovation to fulfil the missions. Creation of dedicated portals, tie-ups with device makers, development of customized products, dissemination of case studies could all add up to a powerful impact. In addition, more open-source technology platforms could provide a great boost to national innovation.

National missions must enable, empower, and enrich the downtrodden and needy members of the society, strengthening the social firmament and must reinforce the competitive and comparative advantages of the nation on par with the best in the world. These objectives require a much larger spread in the industry and the economy. Network communities must channel themselves into dedicated missions as well as target groups to achieve optimal impact.

Nation building cannot be a onetime initiative in time. It has to be a continuous movement. Also, each positive change must be institutionalized and new changes systemically integrated.

CHAPTER-XI

Status Of Political Parties In Social Media

The advent of social media has changed the way information is shared and to certain extents, how it is perceived. The new informational tool is more in line with the core ethos of a democracy than traditional media tools. It is truly, 'of the people, by the people, for the people'. It was a matter of time before the vast potential of this new medium became apparent to the political parties in India but when it did, the campaign strategy of the parties began to be tailored to fit into the 140 characters. The platform of two-way interaction it provided as opposed to the stale and monologues propagation of traditional campaigning began to be utilized by the parties and leaders to sense the mood of their constituents in real time. The first indication of the power of 'Tweets' and 'likes' was the unprecedented success of Aam Aadmi party in the assembly elections of Delhi conducted in December 2013. Riding on the momentum the party has gathered by and large through the well thought out and handsomely executed social media strategy, AAP secured 28 seats on its debut. With the upcoming general elections in 2014, the timelines of twitter and Facebook became the battleground on which war of hash tags, tweets, likes and shares became a regular feature. The parties began to chalk out the best possible strategies in order to engage the voters especially the first-time voters numbering more than 100 million large chunks of which was active on the social media.

An important question is canning social media really make a difference in political campaigning? Do likes and tweets mean votes on the ground? These questions are not easy to answer. A study by Bangalore-based simplify-360 found that 31 percent of Twitter users in India read a tweet on politics. The reporter further suggests that there is a presence of 24 percent of Indian voters on social media which is a key factor in determining the poll results because 2.6 crore Indians read tweets related to elections.

Another report by IAMAI and IRIS knowledge Foundation shows that of India's 543 constituencies, 160 can be termed as 'high impact'- that is, susceptible to the influence of social media. Furthermore, 67 constituencies are categorized as medium impact, 60 as low-impact and 256 as no-impacts constituencies.

The results of the General elections seem to have answered some of the questions but also have raised few new ones. Why despite the perceptible dominance of AAP on social media and the buzz it created, it ended up with mere 4 seats? Even though the clear majority obtained by the BJP somewhat adheres to the equation of 'tweets=votes' the relatively low percentage of votes (31%) it received obscure the clear picture.

This report overviews and analyses the social media standing of the main three parties (BJP, Congress & AAP) and the strategies adopted by these parties in the months leading up to the General elections-2014. The statistics provided in this report are of the period prior to the May-14 elections and do not represent the current social media standing of the Parties.

The Saffron surge: Bhartiya Janta Party

The one thing that was ominous to the leaders opposing BJP Prime ministerial candidate Narendra Modi in 2014 General elections, was that the man enjoyed unparallel support on social media. Since Nehru, no political leader had this kind of support from the masses. The phenomenon was neither spontaneous nor entirely volunteer based. As opposed to party, on social media the relentless campaign for Modi was person-centric way before he was formerly elected the PM candidate by BJP. The then Gujarat CM, due to the perceived partiality of conventional media, especially English channels, or so he believed, left him no alternative but to address the people directly and SM came as a boon for the wily leader.

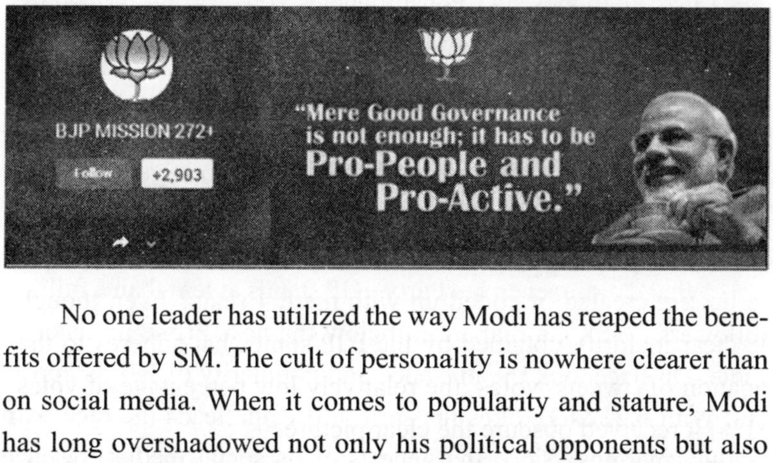

No one leader has utilized the way Modi has reaped the benefits offered by SM. The cult of personality is nowhere clearer than on social media. When it comes to popularity and stature, Modi has long overshadowed not only his political opponents but also his comrades in the BJP and the BJP itself. Even a cursory glance at the stats of SM reveals an interesting picture. Narendra Modi is unarguably the most popular Indian leader on social media with 6.06 million followers on Twitter, **20,912,172** 'Likes' on Facebook in addition to his personal blog and websites (as of August 2014).

Now compare it to the opposition. The most popular Congress leader on Twitter is Shashi tharoor with 2.32 million followers and Arvind Kejriwal of Aam Aadmi party has 2.28 million followers. The differences become starker on Facebook where most popular Congress leader is Omen Chandy, Chief Minister of Kerala with half a million likes. As far as other Congress leaders are concerned, Dr Manmohan Singh has a total of 463,011 likes, while Congress Vice President Rahul Gandhi has 360,454 and former union minister and Thiruvananthapuram Lok Sabha member Shashi Tharoor has 235,343. According to Follower Wonk, Narendra Modi's social authority is 86 (on the scale of 1-10; where 1 is lowest and 100 is highest).

What's more, even his Party, BJP stands at less than a million followers (738K), a mark well below the now Prime minister of India. On Facebook the presence and popularity of BJP is apparent. With **6,222,632** likes the saffron brigade leads the race with healthy margins. Since the genesis of its social media presence back in October 2010, BJP has dominated the virtual space and has been rewarded handsomely well in this regard.

A look at Facebook's top Indian trends in 2013 reveals that Narendra Modi, th then PM candidate of BJP is the most talked about person on Facebook, beating personalities such as Indian cricket legend Sachin Tendulkar and RBI governor Raghuram Rajan. Even India's Mars mission failed to generate as much buzz as Narendra Modi did. The majority of Facebook's 82 million Indian MAUs (Monthly active users) seemed to be hooked to the then CM of Gujarat.

The reason for the stunning success of persona of Narendra Modi and by extension of BJP on social media can be attributed to several aspects. Focus on direct interaction, inclusive campaigning, sound strategy and the reluctance of its competitors helped the saffron brigade in dominating the new-age media, which is the social media.

The Battle Plan 2014

"The defeats in the years 2004 and 2009, led to the evolution of Bhartiya Janta Party as a stronger and more accomplished political party, which focuses equally on the conventional and the new age tactics for election campaigning. The party opted for a more far-reaching shift in their approach by prognostic Growth and Development as the key agenda".

The multi-phased strategy of BJP was carefully outlined with the sole aim of obtaining 272+ seats in the General Elections of 2014. "Between 2010 and 2012 the strategy was to connect with the internet savvy generation on social networks. After 2012, the party laid out a twin strategy of bringing more and more people on Party's social media platforms and simultaneously creating an interest and the desire to stay connected by opening up the doors of IT cell, India 272+ and various other volunteer communities". In this way the two-way communication was improved, providing the volunteers a sense of pride as the social media warriors of BJP.

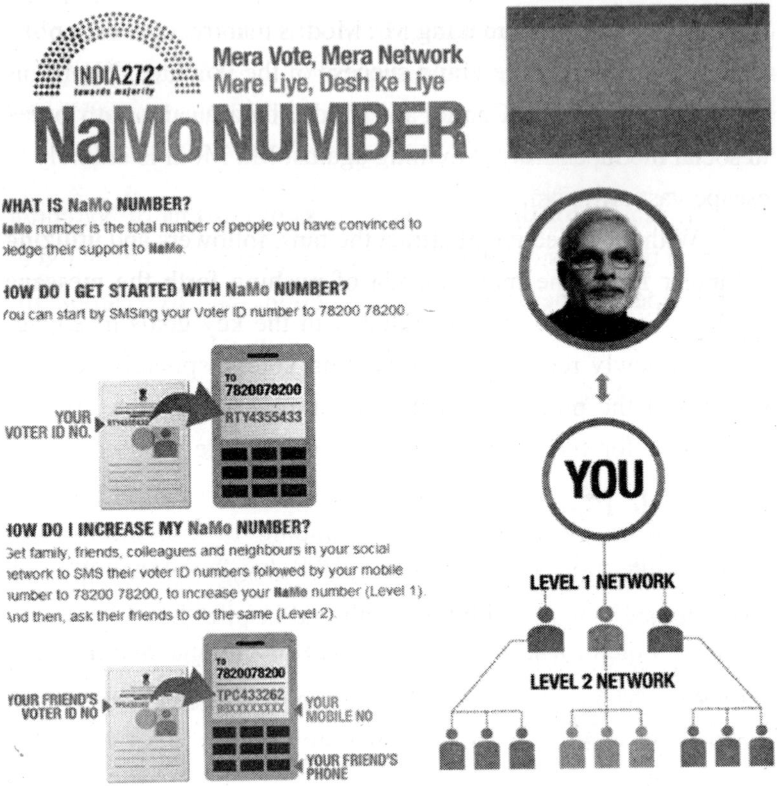

BJP is leaving nothing to chance and seems to be the Party which has truly grasped the potential benefits social media has to offer. The Modi machine is constantly testing new instruments to influence voters. On Holi, Mr. Modi sent personalised Direct Messages to thousands of people with a signed photograph for each of them. Unlike a regular Direct Message, this was connected to a link that enabled the receivers to tweet or share the autographed image. It was something never done before, forcing someone to say: "won't vote for Modi but impressed with his digital campaign." Not just this, Mr. Modi has also forced his team to up his presence on WhatsApp and SMS in addition to the social media blitzkrieg. Even the 'chai pe charcha' campaign is a social media seed, making Mr. Modi's mantra: connect online and engage offline. The grand success of the volunteer platforms such as India272, Niti Central and Modi Bharasa can be attributed to social media entirely. Anything against Mr. Modi is unlikely to escape vast criticism.

"With the objective of attract the fans, followers and utilizing volunteer force, the main agenda of pushing forth the message of 'Vote For BJP' was constituted with the key goals of engaging with newly registered and existing voters, spreading awareness about the party's agenda and campaigns, generate interest and desire for the party's initiatives and future prospects, register growth, development, alternative for change with party's name with keywords- Nurture a community of Brand Advocates for the party, integrate offline-online campaigns to broaden the spectrum and engage with the youth and inspire them to contribute their bit towards the mission. BJP has remained the front-runner in the race under the leadership of Shri Narendra Modi when it came to social media marketing strategy. While other political parties were still working on the initial stages of online community, BJP already created a huge community of fans, followers and subscribers duly allowing them a mass presence across virtual world." (http://www.socialsamosa.com/2014/03/social-media-strategy-review-bharatiya-janta-party)

"The party used an intelligent mix of digital advertising, public relations and content marketing to create a community of advocates who interact, discuss and share the prospects of voting for BJP with millions of users across various social media platforms leading to a state of positive word of mouth. They key aspect of the strategy was the flawless integration in content strategy for different platforms right from Facebook to

Twitter, Google+, India 272+, Youtube, Whatsapp and other platforms. The content remained relevant and original for the online audience with the strategy of being at the right place, at the right time, with the right message, to the right people. Each post has a logical connect and extension which further enunciates BJP's proposition towards growth, development and good governance". (http://www.socialsamosa.com/2014/05/social-media-strategy-review-comparison-parties-social-media/)

Twitter

"On Twitter, BJP was in the dominating position since the very beginning. The common trends on Twitter for BJP were BJPor #NaMoinHP or NaMo in City such as #NaMoInLucknow. By relentless tweeting campaign, thousands of tweets were posted everyday with #NamoBJP, #NaMo4PM and so on. The tone and the theme of communication was on the lines of Facebook and the numbers of contributors increased manifold". (http://www.socialsamosa.com/2014/05/social-media-strategy-review-comparison-parties-social-media/)

On Twitter, BJP gave a live commentary of events along with posts of spreading awareness about voting in elections, complementing offline events, seeking donations, sharing greetings, displaying growth facts, membership calls, quotes from prominent leaders, retweets from leaders, members, volunteers and third-party information sources.

Since Twitter is all about real time conversation, the focus of the party here is on giving it a human touch in all forms of messaging. The pictures shared are aimed to stir the emotional instinct of the audience. "The party has been able to trend almost every hash tag connecting with Narendra Modi's rally in a particular city or region. Surprisingly every trend has new contributors to support the trend; with the trending hashtag the party connects with new users and followers on Twitter everyday. One other essential factor of the party's efforts on Twitter is the smooth availability of content and volunteers who support the party's stand over issues". (http://www.socialsamosa.com/2014/03/social-media-strategy-review-bharatiya-janta-party)

"These are homogeneous channels to publicize information which comes handy in online discussions. For instance, at the time of Rahul Gandhi's visit to Gujarat on 8th Feb 2014 for a rally BJP managed to trend #RGExposesBJP from morning hours till afternoon, wherein they branded the figures of Gujarat as lies but Namo supporters were quickly hijacked the trend, posting replies to accusations and in a couple of hours #NaMoinImphal and #NaMoin Manipur started trending on Twitter". (http://www.socialsamosa.com/2014/03/social-media-strategy-review-bharatiya-janta-party)

"This demonstrates the strength of BJP and its supporters on Twitter. On Twitter, apart from #NaMo in a particular city hash tag, the party has extensively used the hash tags of 360-degree campaigns like #MereSapnonKaBharat, #ChaiPeCh archa which received an overwhelming response of as much as 40,000 tweets in a day". (http://www.socialsamosa.com/2014/03/social-media-strategy-review-bharatiya-janta-party)

"As per the MTS election tracker, the engagement on Twitter, in recent times, has received certain spikes at regular intervals, like on 23rd Feb the levels shot up due to Narendra Modi's Fateh Rally in Punjab; on 27th of Feb Narendra Modi – A victim of manipulations book was released, along with the first list of candidates contesting the Lok Sabha Elections; on 1st of March engagement levels rose again as Ex-Army General VK

Singh joined BJP #Fauji4Modi was trending that day; accordingly on 3rd, #NamoinBihar was trending leading to an increase in the engagement levels. On 5th of March, with the announcement of poll dates, the engagement levels for the party's Twitter handle shot up for quite some time". (http://www.socialsamosa.com/2014/03/social-media-strategy-review-bharatiya-janta-party)

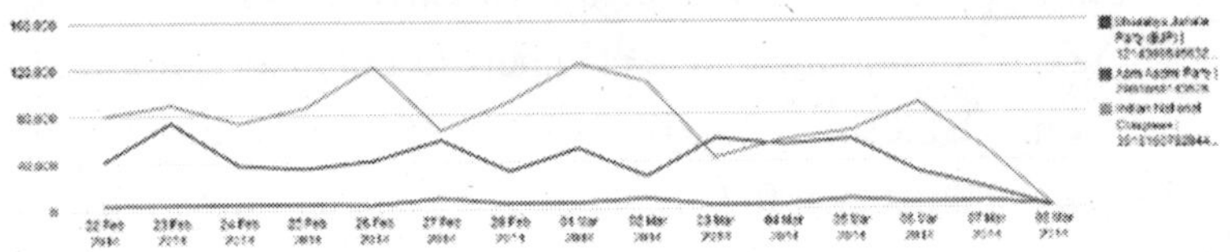

The engagement levels of BJP4India activities on Twitter are lower than AAP. "The reason behind this remains the same as AAP manages to concentrate all of their communication around the Aam Aadmi Party Twitter handle and Arvind Kejriwal BJP has scattered and divergent synergies in place, this approach definitely adds to the reach and timeline deliveries for keywords associated to BJP, as a result, the engagement levels for BJP4India that is i.e., the official Twitter handle suffer a jolt". (http://www.socialsamosa.com/2014/03/social-media-strategy-review-bharatiya-janta-party)

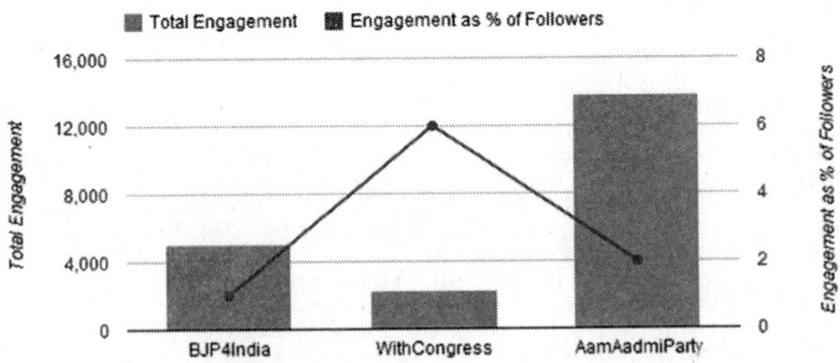

A comparison of engagement levels on Twitter

Facebook

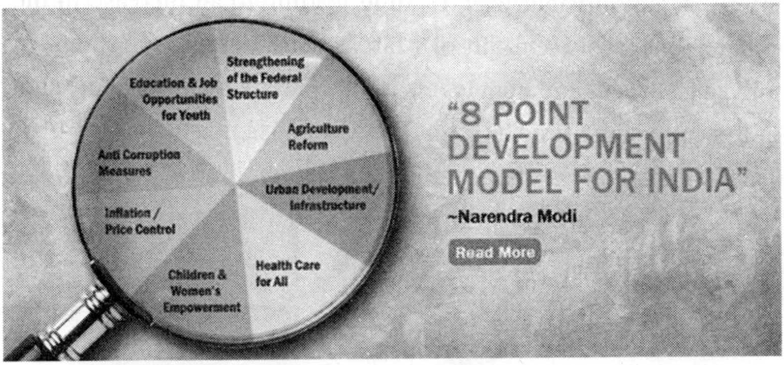

The Facebook campaign of BJP and the communication style it has adopted has two main agendas; "covering an array of things from proposing models of development in India to debunking the claims of growth and development under the UPA regime. The posts also include tributes to legends, greetings on several occasions, live coverage of events, info-graphics of the next rally/campaign, and videos of prominent leaders like Narendra Modi, Rajnath Singh, Arun Jaitley and Sushma Swaraj". (http://www.socialsamosa.com/2014/05/social-media-strategy-review-comparison-parties-social-media/)

BJP utilized Facebook ads with targeted demographics to increase the number of fans and increase the engagement levels. Several contests and campaigns are undertaken by the party to engage with the existing fans. "Such as, Mere Sapnon ka Bharat, where the users are supposed to record and upload their vision for India and the best entries stand a chance to meet Narendra Modi in person. Yuva Quiz was conducted by the party to interact with fans on Facebook. BJP launched one of the biggest digital on-ground activations in India – Chai Pe Charcha – with the help of CAG, wherein users could ask, share or suggest their views and opinions on the theme by posting on Facebook as well". (http://www.socialsamosa.com/2014/03/social-media-strategy-review-bharatiya-janta-party)

Facebook was utilized as a donation seeking platform by the party, asking supporters to contribute for Change. The #Modi4PM Fund app for donation is hosted on the official website as well on the Facebook page. Similar posts and graphics were run as ads on Facebook and Google Display networks.

"The engagement stats for the party on Facebook are only the one side of the picture and as the social media strategy revolves around Narendra Modi most of the engagement on Facebook happens on his page". (http://www.socialsamosa.com/2014/03/social-media-strategy-review-bharatiya-janta-party).

Youtube

Long before Party's official debut on video sharing website, Narendra Modi had recognized its potential and debuted on YouTube in 2007 on the day of Baba Saheb Ambedkar's birthday. "The YouTube channel for the party was started in 2010 has a collection of 5000+ videos. The channel has 44,685 subscribers, with 62 million views registered. The nature of the videos shared on YouTube is varied including Women's' Day and Voters' Registration Day, videos of press conferences from distinguished speakers, speeches from Shri Narendra Modi, Q&A sessions with prominent leaders, calls for donation, videos clarifying the party's stand over issues of national importance, coverage of several events and as such". (http://www.socialsamosa.com/2014/03/social-media-strategy-review-bharatiya-janta-party)

Engagement levels on YouTube are reasons for this success. "The main reason is that BJP4India is the only channel, other Narendra Modi's official channel, for communication, so all the synergies are converged towards a single focal point" (http://www.socialsamosa.com/2014/03/social-media-strategy-review-bharatiya-janta-party).

In addition, the videos and other contents are optimized and designed to suit the needs of prospective target audience. "BJP seems to understand the vitality of the medium so well that over the time party has started posting videos which answer the queries of subscribers like, Why BJP? How to contribute for change?". (http://www.socialsamosa.com/2014/03/social-media-strategy-review-bharatiya-janta-party)

"The videos posted on the channel were not only visually and aesthetically appealing but party attempted to inject emotional elements and a certain sense of attachment through these videos, be it Narendra Modi's speeches or the call for women empowerment video, or the Modi aane wala hai video song". (http://www.socialsamosa.com/2014/05/social-media-strategy-review-comparison-parties-social-media/). The videos posted connected with the masses on account of emotional appeal.

India 272+ Portal and App

This is a pioneering and innovative initiative by the BJP's social media team. "It is an online volunteering platform to help the BJP in its mission towards gaining more than 272 seats out of 545 in Lok Sabha. The idea for India 272+ was derived from Obama's presidential campaign, where the volunteers and supporters were provided a dashboard to connect, collaborate and contribute their efforts. The India 272+ website has an easy to user interface; users can register using their Facebook/Twitter profile. Even the login facility is through social connect which gives them access to social data. The website has been the battle ground for quite a lot of campaigns run by the party". (http://www.socialsamosa.com/2014/03/social-media-strategy-review-bharatiya-janta-party).

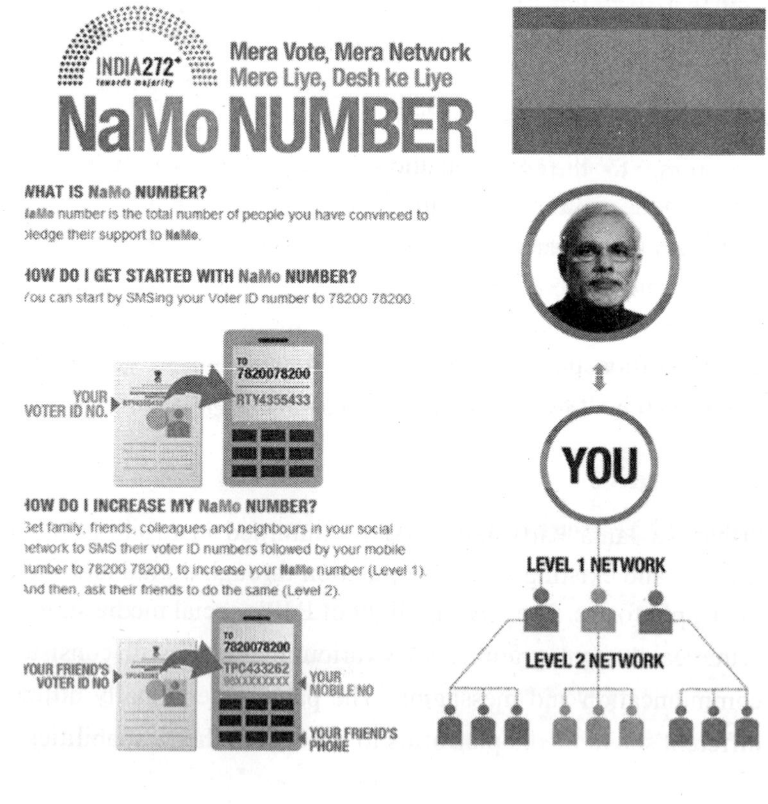

The Impact

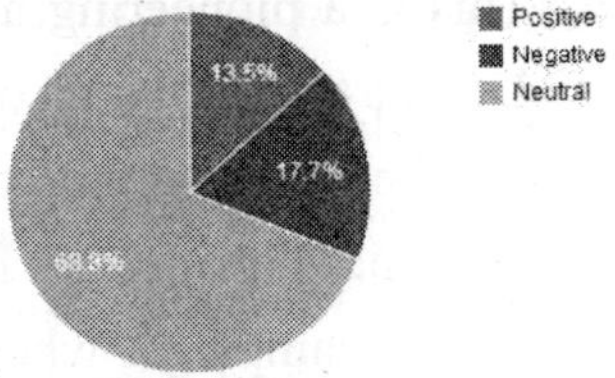

"When looking at the online sentiment by date for the party in the specific 15 days period it is evident that the negative sentiment was the highest on 5th and 6th of March because of the denial from Narendra Modi to meet Arvind Kejriwal which resulted in a spat between supporters of the party in Delhi as well as in Gujarat.

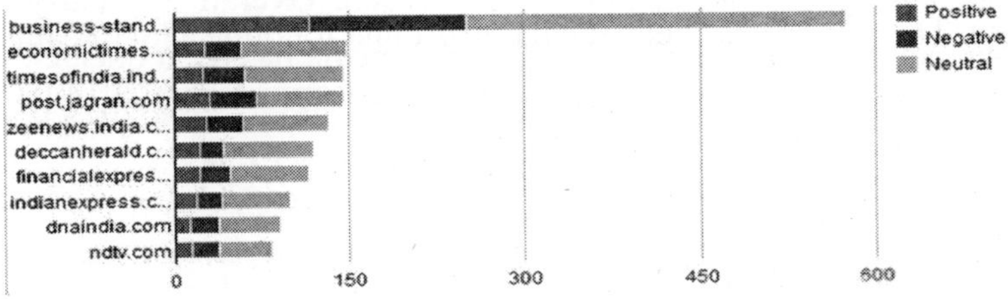

User sentiment stats: BJP

According to the MTS election tracker, Bhartiya Janta Party achieved a neutral to positive sentiment online. The neutral sentiment amounts to 68.8%, positive sentiment is close to 13.5% and the negative sentiment is 17.7%. The negative sentiment can be attributed to the supporters and followers of the opposition parties". (http://www.socialsamosa.com/2014/03/social-media-strategy-review-bharatiya-janta-party)

The Verdict

"Bhartiya Janta Party left no stone unturned in reaching out to the new and existing voters' population through digital and social media platforms. The key highlight of BJP's social media strategy is the seamless integration across various platforms with consistent communication and messaging. The party exceptionally utilized different social media platforms to the best of their capabilities.

Mentions on prominent digital publications

The party launched some exceptionally innovative campaigns and initiatives like Mere Sapnon Ka Bharat, Namo Number, Chai Pe Chacha to register their presence synonymous with Growth, Development and Good Governance. BJP on social media reached the pinnacle point, wherein, the stage is set for them to engage with the users and gain votes by tangible conversions. The brilliant Offline-Online Integration of the party's activities helped the party in expanding their reach. Overall, the party's approach towards the digital and social media has been outstanding and impressive". (http://www.socialsamosa.com/2014/03/social-media-strategy-review-bharatiya-janta-party).

The Sweep: Aam Aadmi Party

In the Delhi assembly election, the stunning performance of AAP was interpreted as the rise of an alternative politics, a political ideology starkly different from the main two parties BJP and Congress. The phenomenal performance and wider reach of the party was greatly attributed to its efficient and aggressive online campaigning. "Aam Aadmi Party has been in the limelight since December 2013, portrayed as having mildly controversial political mottos by Indian media. The leader of the party, Mr. Arvind Kejriwal, established the Aam Aadmi Parti in November 2012 and was elected CM of Delhi in the very first election fought by them in 2013".(http://www.socialsamosa.com/2014/03/social-media-strategy-review-aam-aadmi-party/)

Strategy, content and objectives

After the Delhi election Aam Aadmi Party emerged as one of the most effective and influential political parties and its decision to fight in the general election on national level were interpreted both as overambitious and unorthodox. The social media strategy they adopted for the General election was not very different from the one that they had experimented with in Delhi. They are following the same strategy on Twitter as well as on Facebook.

The Party has four main objectives:

- Plug in their honest opinions and reach the masses.
- Spread awareness about party movements
- Display a common voice, in line with offline objectives
- Connect with the youth

The focus of the party seems to be on a two-way interaction as opposed to traditional political campaigning of propaganda and one way flow of information. "They are using social media as an outlet to talk to their fans and followers. The party is also influencing and shaping the thoughts of online users to their advantage by using motivational images and strong content. AAP has proved far more successful on Twitter as compared to Facebook". (http://www.socialsamosa.com/2014/03/social-media-strategy-review-aam-aadmi-party/). The nature of audience on Twitter seems perfectly suitable for a political party.

On Facebook, the political party has a similar strategy. Sharing of videos exposes the work that AAP has been carrying out and it is posted regularly.

Twitter

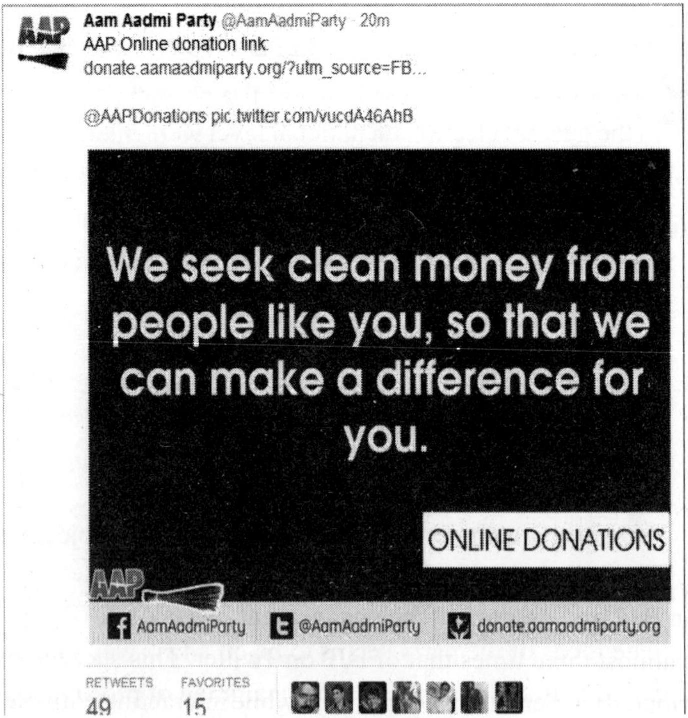

"AAP's campaign strategy on Twitter is to use hash-tags effectively, raise the issues, voice the common grievances and run a certain campaign for specific time periods. For example, during the Kanpur rally, they used #KejriwalAtKanpur and kept their fans from across the country updated about every move". (http://www.socialsamosa.com/2014/03/social-media-strategy-review-aam-aadmi-party/). Frequently, AAP's hashtags have clashed with BJP's, for instance #KejriwalAtKanpur was trending and was in competition with #NamoInLucknow. "Though there were mixed reviews from Twitter users about Kejriwal's Kanpur visit, it was definitely in line with their overall strategy. Also, it drove engagement with controversial topics that cropped up at the rally". (http://www.socialsamosa.com/2014/03/social-media-strategy-review-aam-aadmi-party/)

The party seems to be more in touch with its target audience than BJP or Congress. "The engagement levels of AAP activities are almost three times that of BJP on Twitter. This success can be attributed to a personalized approach while interacting with users on

Twitter. The political party uses a common voice rather than relentlessly indulging in self-promotion". (http://www.socialsamosa.com/2014/03/social-media-strategy-review-aam-aadmi-party/)

Facebook

As compared to Twitter, The Party seemed to be behind on Facebook. Indian National Congress and BJP are way ahead of AAP. While Congress is engaging with 60% of its fanbase, AAP is only at 4.81%. Though, given the nature of Facebook promotions which can be bought, the numbers may not be portraying the true picture.

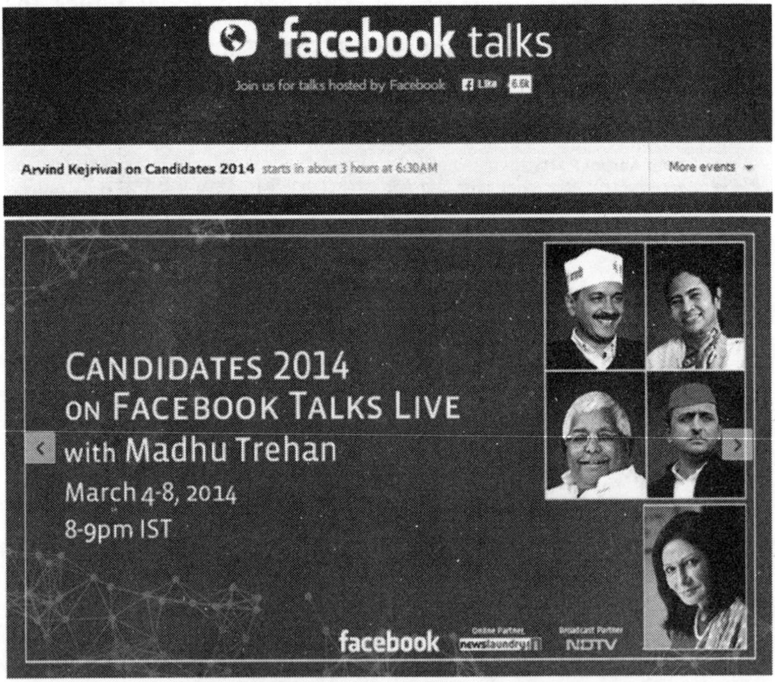

Arvind Kejriwal on Candidates 2014

Facebook partners with newslaundry.com and NDTV to bring you a multi-platform Town Hall Event with leading political contenders.

Although "Aam Aadmi Party has quickly ramped up its Facebook fan count, the party can do better with its page. Simply posting the same content on both Facebook and Twitter does not serve any purpose. If Twitter is being used for awareness, Facebook can be used for chats with spokespersons of the party or launch powerful campaigns to boost party objectives". (http://www.socialsamosa.com/2014/03/social-media-strategy-review-aam-aadmi-party/)

The Perception

The sentiment in engagement would best describe what users on Twitter feel about AAP's campaigns. According to the MTS election tracker, "on 2nd March when the #KejriwalAtKanpur campaign was executed, there was a decrease in negative sentiments. On 22nd February 2014, the Twitter handle had the maximum negative sentiment, precisely because of the attack on AAP volunteers by the NCP. This act was condemned by the online users. The MTS election tracker shows that Twitter mentions of AAP reached 4,555, highest in comparison with BJP and Congress". (http://www.socialsamosa.com/2014/03/social-media-strategy-review-aam-aadmi-party/)

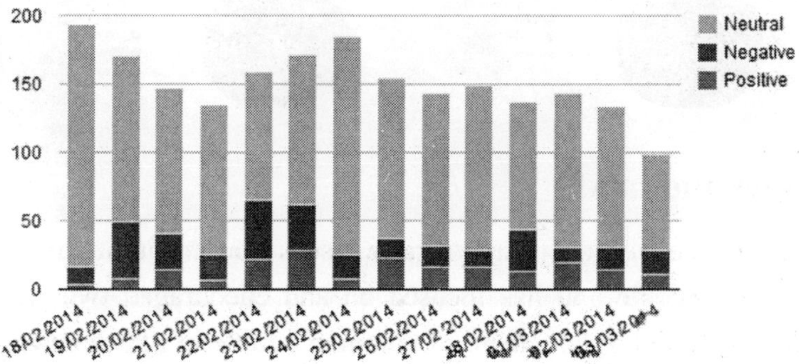

Sentiments:

The Website

This communication is also consistent with their website. "The website entry page talks about online donations. There is also an application to promote the same. The donation trends on the party's website show that the party is highly motivated to showcase each day's donation count and the breakup of the same. It is an intelligent idea to promote donations through social media especially because it is the best way to display to a common man each day's collection details, hence encouraging them to be a part of the collection". (http://www.socialsamosa.com/2014/03/social-media-strategy-review-aam-aadmi-party/) The spiking donation stats over the course of the campaign, especially when the Party came under attack seem to support this notion.

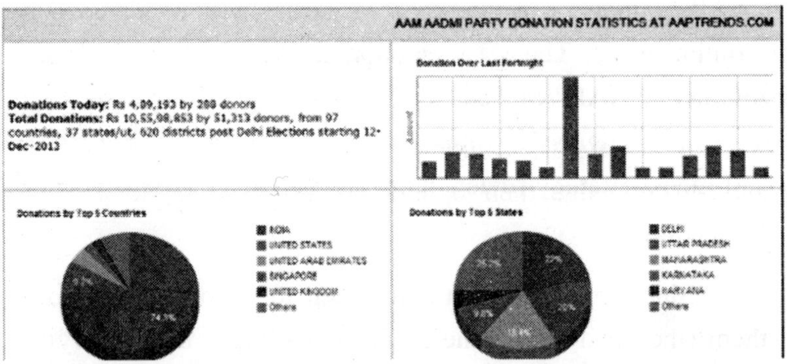

Issues and talks

AAP has consistently tried to raise issues that are important to common people and has focused on and encouraged two way interaction and involvement of common people in the campaign and party's online activities. The #Internship4AAP also suggests that there is an open invitation for students to join the movement and again supports transparency in objectives. The huge volunteer base of AAP seems to testify for the success of this campaign. (User reply ratio graph, below)

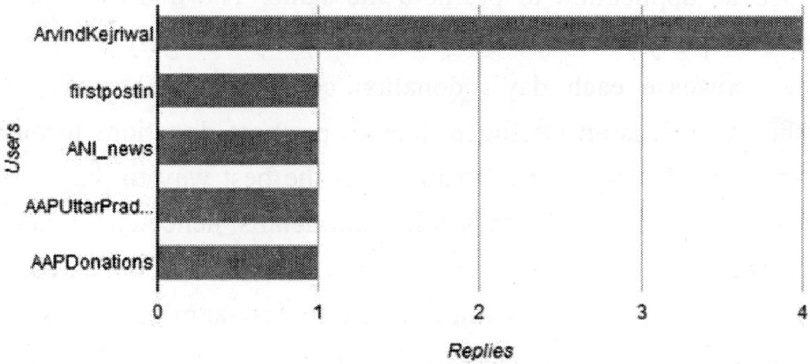

The issue of Reliance was openly taken up by AAP on Twitter, again, "a very apparent approach in bringing facts in front of the country. However, where AAP is attempting to put facts ahead of the people through Twitter, they became unresponsive to the replies on such tweets which go entirely against the purpose of the platform. The political party must respond to user tweets and acknowledge their opinion as has been claimed by their leadership".

"Since the party claims to listen to people and respond to them (they had even gone as far as calling a meet every week at one of Delhi's busiest roads, where the CM would openly listen to them), not responding on Twitter does not help their objectives". (http://www.socialsamosa.com/2014/03/social-media-strategy-review-aam-aadmi-party/)

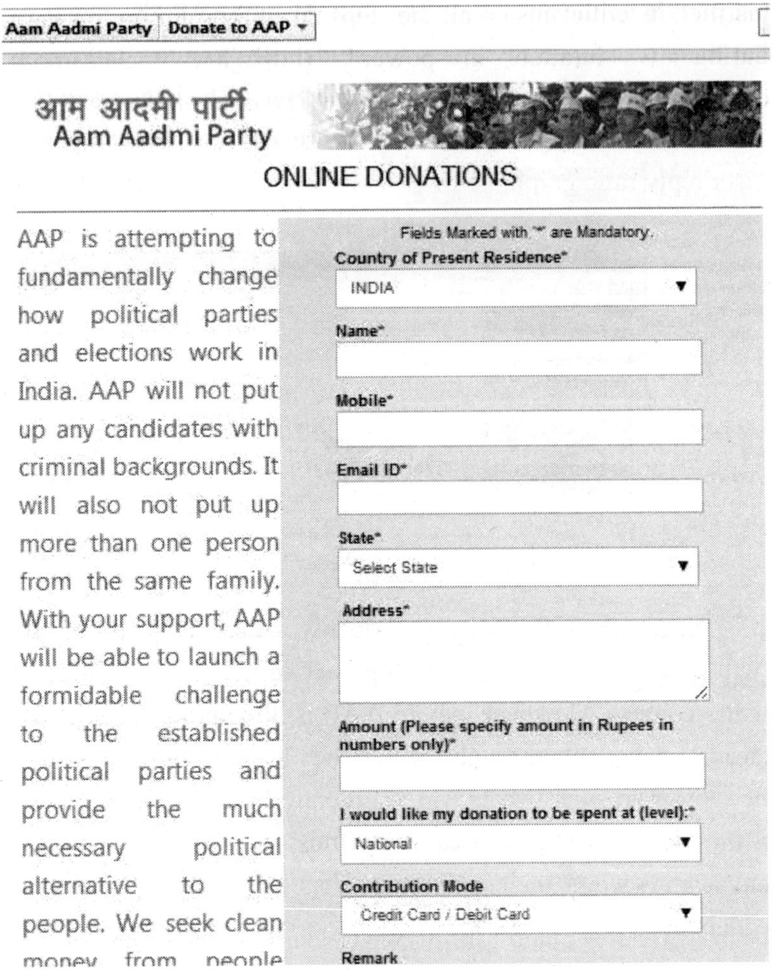

The Mentions

AAP has been consistently mentioned by the major Digital publications including Business Standard, Times of India and Economic Times. Regrettably, "all the websites have more negative mentions about the party and less positive mentions. Business Standard has been condemning AAP of its activities and closely tracking all movements. The magazine even criticized and justified its criticisms on all the steps taken by Aam Aadmi Party during its duration in power". (http://www.socialsamosa.com/2014/03/social-media-strategy-review-aam-aadmi-party/)

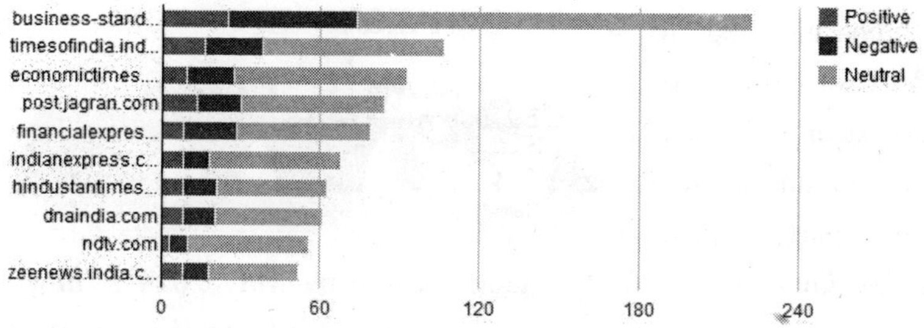

Mentions on Digital publications

The Verdict

As the late entrant to the party, "AAP is making every successful attempt through social media to reach the first-time young voter. What goes in the favor of this political outfit is the transparency and knack for engagement it has displayed. With various proactive details of the party moves and transparent behavior on social media, it is acting as a vehicle to collect vote banks. The brilliant mix of offline field work for the rural classes and the perfect social media strategy for the online educated youngsters the party is sure-footed". (http://www.socialsamosa.com/2014/03/social-media-strategy-review-aam-aadmi-party/).

Indian National Congress on social media

In the General Assembly elections held in 2009, "206 Congress candidates got elected to the 543-member house as a result Congress led coalition of political parties called the United Progressive Alliance (UPA) was able to gain a majority and form the government. The party in the recent times is facing criticism masses over allegations of widespread corruption, inflation, economic turmoil which has led to the formation of a strong negative factor against the party prior

to the General Assembly Elections due by May 2014". (http://www.socialsamosa.com/2014/04/social-media-strategy-review-indian-national-congress/)

"The Indian National Congress founded in 1885, is by far the largest and one of the oldest democratically operating political parties in the world. The party's modern liberal platform is largely considered to be on the Centre-left of the Indian political spectrum in contrast to the right-wing Bharatiya Janta Party".

(http://www.socialsamosa.com/2014/04/social-media-strategy-review-indian-national-congress/)

It is rather surprising that the party which apparently claims to represent the youth remained away from social media for years. After ignorance and apparent disregard, the Congress Party realized the fact that in order to reach to the younger generation the party must embrace the social media. "While the opposition Bharatiya Janta Party and Aam Aadmi Party have effectively utilized the importance and relevance of social media for connecting with the masses, engaging with them using a 360 degree approach the Congress party used very simple and straight forward strategy on social media". (http://www.socialsamosa.com/2014/04/social-media-strategy-review-indian-national-congress/)

"The Congress party started with organized and planned social media operations in mid-2013 after realizing that in the race to win over netizens in India. Congress joined the social media bandwagon by launching a Facebook page, a twitter handle, reworking the website, YouTube channel, volunteers platform Khidkee, WhatsApp and line extensions". (http://www.socialsamosa.com/2014/04/social-media-strategy-review-indian-national-congress/)

Aims

"The party's communication online aimed towards creating a culture of positive, polite and dignified engagement over serious political issues. The volunteers and supporters for the party on social media were instructed to keep the social media discourse respectful. Additionally, they were instructed that every Congress supporter should reject abuse, not by returning that, but by countering it with facts". (http://www.socialsamosa.com/2014/04/social-media-strategy-review-indian-national-congress/)

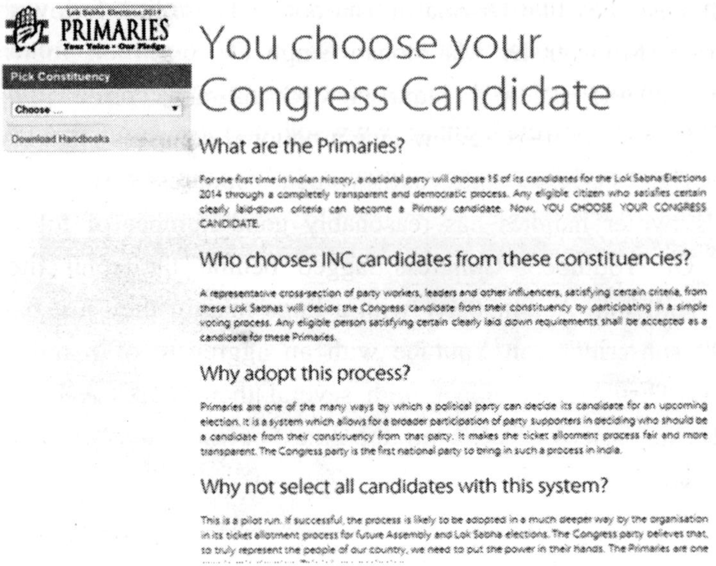

PRIMARIES

Pick Constituency

Choose ...

Download Handbooks

You choose your Congress Candidate

What are the Primaries?

For the first time in Indian history, a national party will choose 15 of its candidates for the Lok Sabha Elections 2014 through a completely transparent and democratic process. Any eligible citizen who satisfies certain clearly laid-down criteria can become a Primary candidate. Now, YOU CHOOSE YOUR CONGRESS CANDIDATE.

Who chooses INC candidates from these constituencies?

A representative cross-section of party workers, leaders and other influencers, satisfying certain criteria, from these Lok Sabhas will decide the Congress candidate from their constituency by participating in a simple voting process. Any eligible person satisfying certain clearly laid down requirements shall be accepted as a candidate for these Primaries.

Why adopt this process?

Primaries are one of the many ways by which a political party can decide its candidate for an upcoming election. It is a system which allows for a broader participation of party supporters in deciding who should be a candidate from their constituency from that party. It makes the ticket allotment process fair and more transparent. The Congress party is the first national party to bring in such a process in India.

Why not select all candidates with this system?

This is a pilot run. If successful, the process is likely to be adopted in a much deeper way by the organisation in its ticket allotment process for future Assembly and Lok Sabha elections. The Congress party believes that, to truly represent the people of our country, we need to put the power in their hands. The Primaries are one

Standing on social in the run-up to General Elections 2014

"In a short span of time Congress managed to build a comprehensive presence across the vital social media networks like Facebook, Twitter, Google+ and YouTube. On Facebook it had 2 million fans with 1.8 million talking about it but still Congress was far behind the principal opposition BJP which had 2.5 million fans. The party had the second highest number of fans on Facebook leading ahead of Aam Aadmi Party which had 1.6 million fans". (http://www.socialsamosa.com/2014/04/social-media-strategy-review-indian-national-congress/)

On Twitter, the INCIndia twitter handle was behind both the competitors with 137,000 followers. This can be attributed to the late beginning of social media journey for the party. "To support the movement for Congress online they had some influential twitter handles like Dr Shashi Tharoor (2.11 million followers) , Prime Minister Dr Manmohan Singh (1.13 million followers) to name a few". (http://www.socialsamosa.com/2014/04/social-media-strategy-review-indian-national-congress/)

The party's state/youth/women congress spokesperson's twitter handles has reasonably good number of followers. On Youtube, "Congress lagged behind the competitors BJP and Aam Aadmi Party with a huge margin they just have 5208 subscribers on Youtube with an aggregate of 8 million views They shared videos with several themes like A Billion and One Voices, TVC's on the lines of their new positioning Har Haath Shakti Har Haath Tarakki, Know your MP and UPA Achievement". (http://www.socialsamosa.com/2014/04/social-media-strategy-review-indian-national-congress/)

"The party regularly posted speeches from Rahul Gandhi, Smt. Sonia Gandhi, PM Manmohan Singh and event coverage from various rallies and interactions organized by state congress units across the country. INC frequently organized webcasts on issues of national importance in association with NIC and Government of India. For example one webcast on theme of Agenda for future, Education and Nation Building was organized on 15th of Feb 2014 , another version of a similar webcast was organized on 26th of Feb 2014. The party also showcased its YouTube channel as INC TV on its website with categories like Economy, History, Politics, Public Affairs, Public values etc". (http://www.socialsamosa.com/2014/04/social-media-strategy-review-indian-national-congress/)

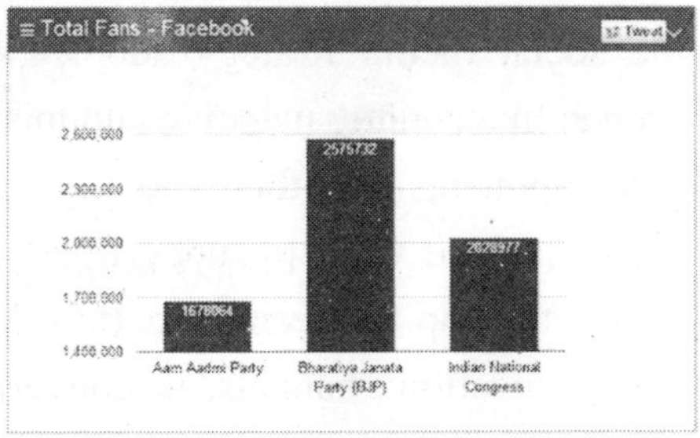

The Indian National Congress Party has the distinction of being the only political party in India to be present on Instagram officially.

Strategy, content and engagement

Since the party was in the Government, the main objective of its campaign was to highlight the achievements of the dispensation and counter the propaganda of the opposition parties. "The Indian National Congress in a reactive approach to the online popularity and reach of opposition party BJP launched well organized and planned social media strategy to meet up these objectives to assist the party in their overall offline campaign prior to General Assembly elections 2014. The party was a bit late to realize that every single voter counts in a fractious electoral democracy like India and 190 million internet users is not a number to be ignored and disdained". (http://www.socialsamosa.com/2014/04/social-media-strategy-review-indian-national-congress/)

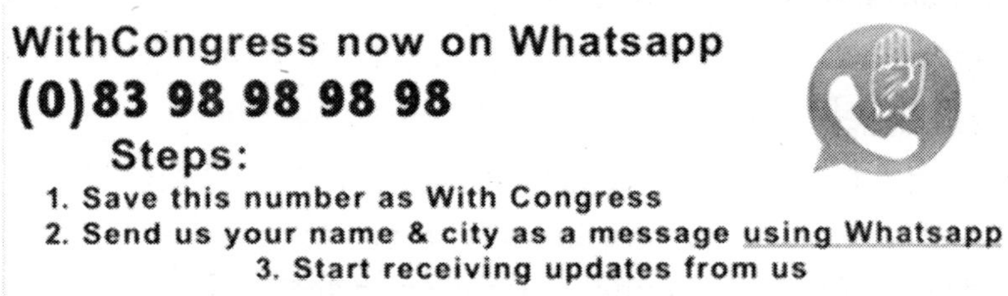

According to Congress spokesperson Priyanka Chaturvedi, the social media strategy adopted by the party had multiples prongs like counter negative and misleading propaganda of political opponents and their mouthpieces, to inform and convince the undecided voter to support party's policies and programs, to bridge the gap between supporters & senior leaders and open up communication channels, to convert supporters into voters and active members of the party, to guide, update and enthuse the core party workers to fulfill political goals of the party.

This multipronged strategy of the party aimed to connect with more people online across various platforms and engage with them in a polite and informed discussion. The basic idea was to reach out to unexplored constituencies where traditionally party has not enjoyed much support. One such initiative was fact check initiative through which the party aims to counter and denounce the claims made by Narendra Modi and BJP.

Before the launch of the social media campaign of the party, Rahul Gandhi made his visions clear. "Congress party stands for Love and Truth. He cited Buddhism as an example and said if individuals in this country have the ability to take the message of peace and nonviolence to countries as far as Japan and South Korea. The Congress party must adopt honest and respectful language even to counter its critics". (http://www.socialsamosa.com/2014/04/social-media-strategy-review-indian-national-congress/)

"The Congress party's approach to social media seems to be very simple and straight forward. The Content Strategy for the party revolves around covering events/rallies as they happen , fact Check to denounce the growth and development claims by Narendra Modi and BJP , powerful quotes extracted from the speeches of Rahul Gandhi, Sonia Gandhi and PM Manmohan Singh, UPA achievements, greetings/testimonials on several occasions, aggressive posts to attack the opposition PM Candidate Narendra Modi. The party's content on Facebook and Google+ is almost similar while the communication on twitter is tailored according to the medium". (http://www.socialsamosa.com/2014/04/social-media-strategy-review-indian-national-congress/)

Facebook

The content strategy on Facebook of the party seems to be propagation of party's ideology, achievements of the government and mobilizing support for Rahul Gandhi. At several points, it seems the whole campaign revolves around exalting the persona of VP Rahul Gandhi. "The cover pictures usually depict a message from the Congress Vice President Mr. Rahul Gandhi or quotes from prominent leaders even agenda for meetings, event pictures, info graphics comparing parameters in NDA and UPA reign are put up as cover pictures. The current cover picture features Rahul Gandhi meeting the youth along with the motto for this year's electoral campaign Voice, Opportunity, Transparency and Empowerment for all". (http://www.socialsamosa.com/2014/04/social-media-strategy-review-indian-national-congress/)

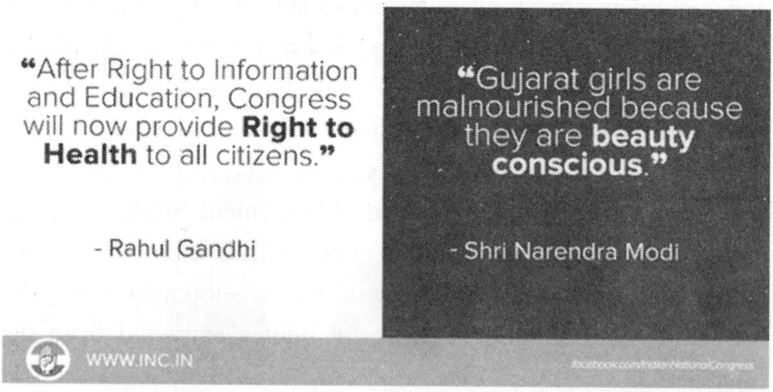

The contents posted were keeping up with the ideology and image of the Congress as pro-poor and secular political organization and frequently evokes the leaders of Nehru-gandhi dynasty as the messiah of poor. The posts carry a tinge of sentimentality in order to connect with the masses. The party's touchy communication tries to connect with the people using an emotional appeal "Policies have to be framed to benefit poor" says Rahul Gandhi along with an album containing pictures of his meet with the rural folks.

"On the other hand, some posts which take potshots at the opposition, comparing the party's brighter prospects and denouncing the claims of development in Gujarat by BJP and Narendra Modi". (http://www.socialsamosa.com/2014/04/social-media-strategy-review-indian-national-congress/)

"The party has come up with a range of initiatives to engage with the people spending their time on Facebook. For example, A Billion and One Voice, UPA Transparency Revolution which talks about the introduction of RTI and how it strives for betterment and excellence in governance. The graphics posted on the page are very neat and classic with the footer for facebook address or Har Haath Shakti Haar Haath Tarakki". (http://www.socialsamosa.com/2014/04/social-media-strategy-review-indian-national-congress/)

The content bucket contains a mix of positive posts, event coverage, aggressive digs at the opposition, tributes, testimonials the form of content also varies from high definition info graphics, print ads, and real time pictures to beautifully crafted videos.

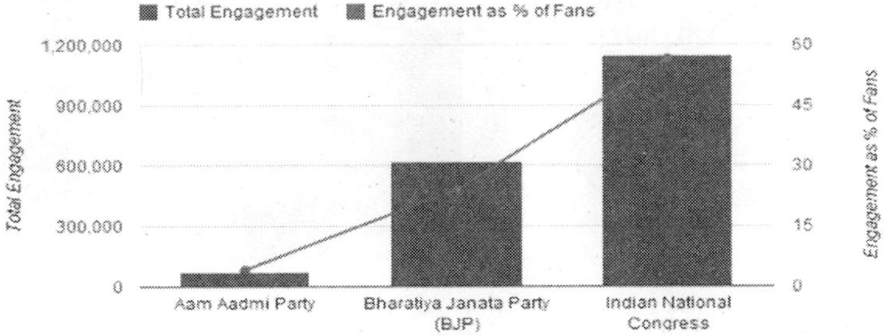

INC FB engagement comparison

"While the Facebook page is sprouting with content with higher engagement numbers the party seems to be underutilizing the community of followers by giving out minimal opportunities for a two way interaction although the INC Manifesto was an interesting way to crowd source suggestions, views and opinions for election manifesto but apart from that there is no major event on Facebook which calls out for participation from the followers". (http://www.socialsamosa.com/2014/04/social-media-strategy-review-indian-national-congress/)

Twitter

Nowhere across the social media platforms the differences and shortcomings of the late entrance of INC is evident better than Twitter. "Indian National Congress on Twitter has less number of followers on Twitter as compared to the opposition but the party has weaved a good network of twitter handles to propagate their message loud and clear". (http://www.socialsamosa.com/2014/04/social-media-strategy-review-indian-national-congress/)

The party is learning to utilize hashtags in an effective way:

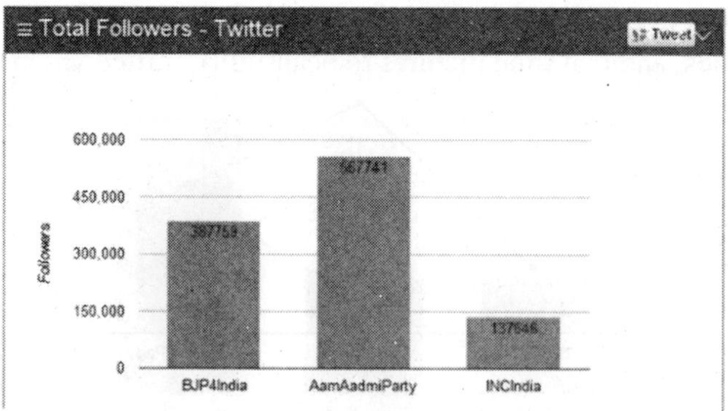

"The hashtag #RGExposesBJP was launched on as a pre cursor to Rahul's rally in Gujarat where in the supporters blatantly criticized Modi and BJP for allegedly false claims regarding Gujarat's development". (http://www.socialsamosa.com/2014/04/social-media-strategy-review-indian-national-congress/). Similarly the #KattarSochNahiYuvaJosh was brilliantly used to cement the youth-leader image of the Congress simultaneously underlining the party's staunchly secular stance.

"Similar to Facebook the party posts on Twitter include fact check on Gujarat and NDA, UPA achievements, impressive quotes from Rahul Gandhi, Smt. Sonia Gandhi and other prominent leaders. Interestingly, Twitter handle for INC India is that they use the promote feature to increase the number of followers. The promote feature is also used for the prominent leaders of the party. The party has also on several occasions managed to hijack trends from the opposition and post content which compares the two". (http://www.socialsamosa.com/2014/04/social-media-strategy-review-indian-national-congress/)

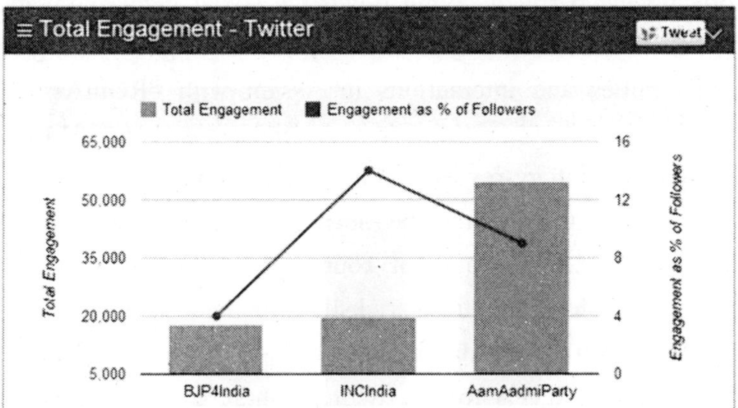

"The party very effectively used hashtags for every rally, interaction featuring Rahul Gandhi with hashtags like #RGinUP, #RGinAssam. Hashtags are used to promote his plans, policies over various issues like education (#RG4Education), soldiers and national security (#RG4Soldiers), peace (#RG4Peace). Rahul Gandhi trends almost every day and was the most mentioned politician for a few days after his frankly speaking interview with Arnab Goswami #RGspeaksArnab". (http://www.socialsamosa.com/2014/04/social-media-strategy-review-indian-national-congress/)

Despite the late entrance, the party was been able to build a community of supporters and volunteers who write in favour of the party and defend the party's stance on twitter. A major portion of Congress' online activity was dedicated to counter the negative propaganda of the opposition by presenting facts and displaying achievements. The party also managed to integrate their twitter campaign online with the offline on ground activity on a couple of occasions thus expanding the reach altogether.

"The engagement levels for the party on twitter have increased manifold. This can be attributed to the sustained efforts by the party in laying down the social media strategy. On 25th of Feb the engagement level was the highest owing to Rahul's rallies and interactions in Assam with #RGinAssam, #RG4Education". (http://www.socialsamosa.com/2014/04/social-media-strategy-review-indian-national-congress/)

"Another spike could be seen on 1st of March when Rahul visited UP for another round of interaction with the common people right from rickshaw pullers to street vendors the #RGinUP during this time frame. On 6th of March, the engagement levels for the twitter handle shot up as Rahul Gandhi visited Mumbai and vernacular #AamchaRahul did a great job in reaching out to the people of Mumbai with fact checks, posts on women empowerment, posts promoting peace and harmony". (http://www.socialsamosa.com/2014/04/social-media-strategy-review-indian-national-congress/)

Youtube

"The Youtube channel for Congress has 5,208 subscribers, with 8 million views registered till date. The Channel is the home to a collection of 512 videos which reiterates the fact that party was too late to start with their social media campaigning. The collection of videos is a wonderful mix including One Billion and a voice series containing stories of people who feel empowered in the 10 year reign of UPA, then there are videos of the TV commercials of the party which emphasize on the new positoning "har haath shakti har haath tarakki". (http://www.socialsamosa.com/2014/04/social-media-strategy-review-indian-national-congress/)

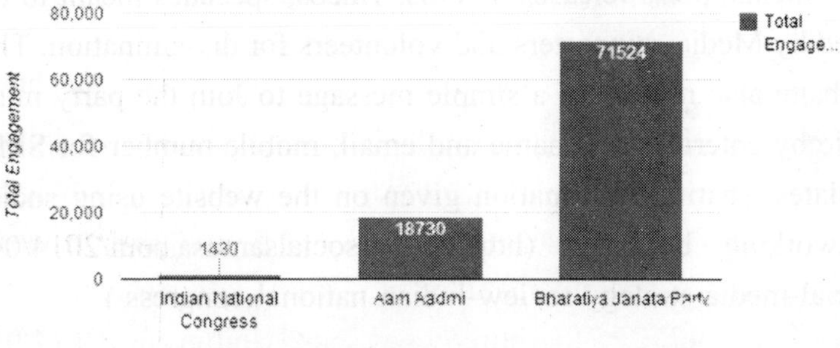

"Excerpts of Rahul Gandhi and Sonia Gandhi's Speeches, videos demystifying the claims of growth and development by Narendra Modi, Videos depicting UPA's achievements , videos talking about youth empowerment , woment empowerment , transparency and Rajiv Gandhi's dream for India, Know your

MP series and so on". (http://www.socialsamosa.com/2014/04/social-media-strategy-review-indian-national-congress/)

INC Website

The official website for Indian National Congress is the hub of all the information regarding the party's campaign online. The website has a simple design layout with options to change languages from English to Hindi/Urdu. The website contains all the information about Congress from its beginning till date, the leaders associated with the party, mission, vision, inspiration and achievements of the party.

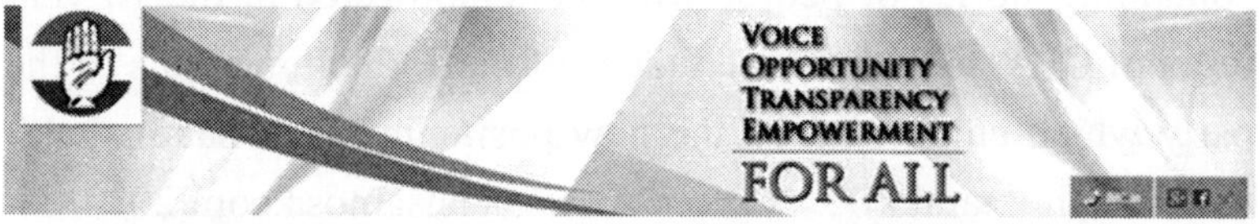

"The website houses a resource section which contains documents, press releases, photos, videos, speeches meant to be used by Media, supporters and volunteers for dissemination. The website also reinforces a simple message to Join the party multiple by entering their name and email, mobile number for SMS updates, sharing information given on the website using social networking buttons". (http://www.socialsamosa.com/2014/04/social-media-strategy-review-indian-national-congress/)

The Perception

"The online sentiment by date for the party in the last 15 days shows that the party has a neutral sentiment on several occasions owing to the spats between AAP and BJP on social media forums. The positive sentiment for the party was highest on 11th March the day when the party executed the trend #KattarSochNahiYuvaJosh". (http://www.socialsamosa.com/2014/04 social-media-strategy-review-indian-national-congress/)

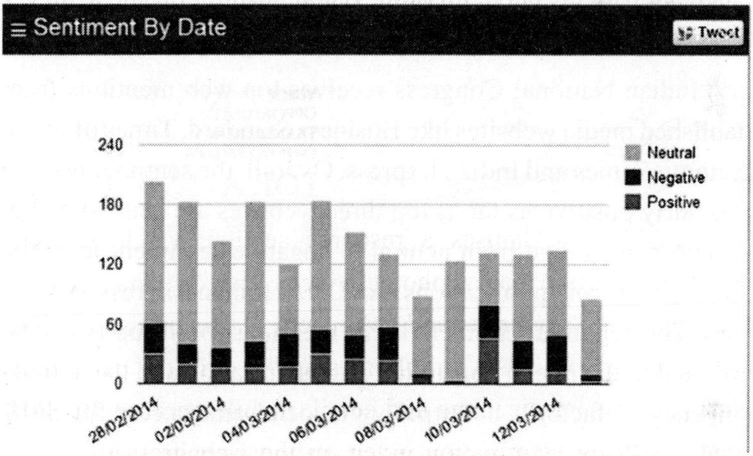

Overall, Indian National Congress Party enjoys a neutral to positive sentiment online. The neutral sentiment amounts to 70.9%, positive sentiment is close to 12.9% and negative sentiment is 16.2%. "Since Social Media is a platform which envisages the right to freedom of speech and expressions due to the equivocal presence of opposition any political party is bound to have a fraction of negative sentiment". (http://www.socialsamosa.com/2014/04/social-media-strategy-review-indian-national-congress/)

Mentions on digital publications

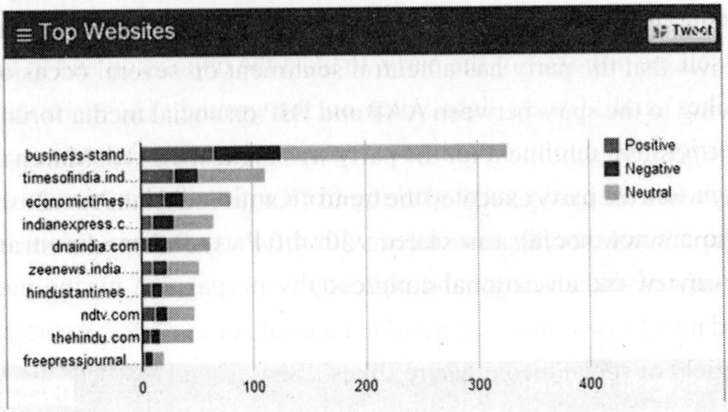

"Indian National Congress receives top web mentions from established media websites like Business Standard, Times of India, Economic Times and Indian Express. Overall, the sentiments seem to be fairly positive as far as top three websites are concerned but the sentiments range from neutral to negative sentiment from the other websites and publications like DNA, Indian Express and Zee News. The negative sentiment in the mentions for the party can be attributed to the rise in corruption scams, inflation and the anti-incumbency factor". (http://www.socialsamosa.com/2014/04/social-media-strategy-review-indian-national-congress/)

"The UPA Government in the recent times has been able to pass Lokpal Bill, Street Vendors Bill, AP Restructure Bill, they have also raised the cylinder cap for a household from 9 to 12 it is because of these welfare reforms the party receives mentions with a positive sentiment". (http://www.socialsamosa.com/2014/04/social-media-strategy-review-indian-national-congress/)

The Timeline Warriors

The power of any campaign, online or offline is determined by the people behind it who create, shape and execute the strategy.

Behind the blitzkrieg unleashed by the political parties on social media, there is a team of professionals working around the clock to sell the promises of the party, to blast the opposition and to turn 'Likes' and 'Tweets' into votes on the ground. These Timeline warriors fall into two distinct categories; the official social media team formed by the party working from within the Party and those who are not directly associated with the Party but are ardent followers of the ideology and philosophy propagated by the party and now have voluntarily assumed the role of crusaders in the battlefield of social media where 'likes' 'Shares' and 'Tweets' are the weapons and opposition party is the enemy which must be eliminated. The majority of the warriors fall into the second category.

According to a report by Mail Today, The IT-Cell of BJP is headed by Arvind Gupta and has 40 members who are mostly professionals from IITs and IIMs working from Party's headquarter, 11 Ashoka Road. There are three large rooms with dozens of computer terminals and laptops where volunteers and professionals were engrossed with the tasks assigned to them. There are several teams that manage aspects such as social media, creative content, donations, and distribution of party material. The volunteer base of BJP is the main strength of this relatively small team. This team designs the strategy the success of which more or less lies in the hands of volunteers.

"At present we have about 45 lakh volunteers and it is surprising that every day more than a lakh volunteers from different parts of the country get attached to the party," said Arvind Gupta, an alumnus of IIT and a PhD from the University of Illinois in the US who heads the BJP's IT wing.

"Our team monitors the activities through phones, internet and various social networking sites," he added.

Gupta said the main purpose of the digital team is strategic readiness for the elections.

"It is like a 360-degree campaign which has been taken beyond the internet in this election. We connect to people through various platforms, including social networking sites like the Facebook and Twitter, and applications like WhatsApp. We also connect through phones. Anybody can have real-time access to Modiji's speech even through phones," he said.

Rajesh Jain and B.G. Mahesh who are not a part of BJP are among those who are rallying behind the cause-Modi by setting up outfits like India272 and Niti Central. Supporting them from the outside are other right-wing social media handles, websites, campaigns, videos etc. set up by Modi fans who are also sometimes dubbed as 'Internet Hindus' due to their far-right political convictions. Twitter handle @Internet_hindus is one such volunteer platform which is dedicated to bash the opposition and even the media outlets if the reports are not favorable.

@Nitinkashyap, @sidgoyal1 are amongst the hundreds of thousands of saffron warriors who are immensely dedicated to BJP and its ideology. @madhukishwar and @swamy39 have contributed much to the popularity of Modi on Twitter.

The phenomenal success of the Aam Aadmi Party in Delhi assembly elections has been variously attributed to the buzz it managed to create on social media. Behind the relentless campaign of the party is informed if rather informal group of volunteers headed by former IT-professional Ankit Lal. Unlike BJP and Congress, even the core social media team of AAP is made up of volunteers who joined the party on the basis of ideology. According to Ankit lal, AAP's focus on positive and clean campaigning as opposed to the mud-slinging apparent in Indian political discourse has been a major factor in attracting educated volunteers for its online activities. The tech-savvy students and young professionals form the backbone of the online volunteer base of the party. The war-room of these warriors is located in Kaushambi, Ghaziabad.

The confusion among ranks was evident in the social media strategy of the Congress Party. Structurally, the party had a very active communication team headed by party general secretary, Ajay Maken, ably supported by party secretary, Priya Dutt, its social media team headed by Deepender Hooda, Research wing headed by Sandeep Dikshit and various spokespersons. However, the incompetency of Party's social media wing was highlighted when it outsourced the marketing campaign aimed to improve the image of Rahul Gandhi on social media in the much hyped and talked about move with a hefty package of INR 500-Crore.

When it comes to volunteers, party lost more than it gained prior to the General elections. Amongst the persistent crusaders for the party were @JhaSanjay and @gsurya along with the 'har hath shakti, har hath tarakki' ad-fame @Hasibaamin.

As the results of 2014 general elections has underlined, the use of social media in today's campaign is critical. The relationship between SNS and politics also has its nodes in the desire for change. SNS will give rise to communities that will massively rise and fall around ideas, not limited by geographical boundaries or languages. Such severely loyal communities can be game-changing for politicians.

CHAPTER XII

Research Study And Analysis

An important burning issue for our society today is the upcoming impact of social networking sites on our youth. A research study for the purpose has been conducted on youths with a view to understand the impact on their lifestyles and also to know the level of consciousness on the community issues like human rights, sexual assaults, women harassment, gender discrimination, environment concerns, political concerns, nation development, etc. For the purpose an empirical comparative study was conducted on 550 people mostly through personal interaction to collect questionnaire for the same from Delhi and Mumbai cities.

Overview of the Research Objectives

- To study the awareness level of usage of different social networking sites.
- To study the purposes for which the SNS's are used.
- To find out level of trust over the information received from social networking sites.
- To determine the likely impact and influence on the lifestyles of Indian youth.
- To study the type of social issues discussed over social networking sites.

To understand the effectiveness of SNS's for social development and nation building.

Hypotheses

1. The Awareness level and usage of SNS are same among the Delhi and Mumbai respondents.
2. Social networking sites do not have any impact and influence on the lifestyles of Indian youth w.r. t the demographic factors (gender, age, education and income).
3. There is no difference in responses from the two cities on the issues of privacy and trust on Sns.
4. There is lack of knowledge on the social networking sites on the social issues discussed.
5. Youth participation is not significant in social development and nation building.

Research methodology

The present research gives an impending approach to the awareness level and the purposes of the SNs of the Indian youth. It also analyses the impact of the networking sites on their lifestyles and how effective they have been on the various social movements like the recent Lok Sabha elections, creating brand identity of leaders and other socio-economic issues like gender discrimination, environment concerns etc. Further, it also identifies the effectiveness of social media for nation development in the times ahead. A questionnaire was administered to collect data for the same and it was analysed using tools like tables, pie-charts, bar graphs, ANOVA and t-test through SPSS version 20.0

The Questionnaire

Keeping in mind the objectives of the study a structured questionnaire was designed. The questionnaire has 23 questions altogether divided into three sections. The sections relates to:

Section I: Personal Information of the respondents

Section II: Types of SNS's and Usage

Section III: Impact and Influence of SNS's

Section I: Personal Information

Section I relates to collecting demographic details of the respondents pertaining to gender, age, educational qualification, category, and income.

Section II: Types of Sns and Usage

This section seeks to obtain responses relating to whether the respondents had accounts on the networking sites, which SNS were more favoured, time spent on them , purposes for which they use and the information about themselves that is provided over these sites.

Section III: Impact and Influence of Sns

Section III contained eleven questions in all, and the responses were rated on a 4-point Likert scale ranging from strongly disagree to strongly agree. This section obtained responses for impact and influence on the lifestyles, level of trust, social issues discussed and the future role of social media.

Sample

A non-probability convenience sampling was used to collect responses from a total of 550 people from Delhi and Mumbai cities. Of which 300 were from Delhi and 250 from Mumbai. No known bias was involved in sampling. Those who could be conveniently approached, were willing to be interacted and are active members of the social networking sites were part of our sample.

The summarized demographic details of the sample are presented below in the table:

Table: Demographic characteristics of the sample

Demographic characteristics		**Delhi (N= 300)**		**Mumbai (N= 250)**		**Total (N= 550)**	
		No.	**%**	**No.**	**%**	**No.**	**%**
Gender	**Males**	168	56 %	132	53 %	300	55 %
	Female	132	44 %	118	47 %	250	45 %
Age	**Below 20 yrs.**	79	26 %	44	18 %	123	22 %
	20 – 30 yrs.	167	56 %	151	60 %	318	52 %
	30 – 40 yrs.	40	13 %	39	16 %	79	18 %
	Above 40 yrs.	14	5 %	16	6 %	30	6 %
Edu. Qualification	**Graduation**	102	34 %	64	26 %	167	34 %
	Post Graduation	125	41 %	106	43 %	231	46 %
	Others	73	25 %	25	32 %	98	20 %

Categ-ory	Student	178	60 %	77	31 %	255	46 %
	Working	75	25 %	138	55 %	213	39 %
	Non-Working	47	15 %	35	14 %	82	15 %
Income	None	102	34 %	72	29 %	174	32 %
	10000-30000	145	48 %	101	40 %	247	45 %
	30000-50000	20	7 %	47	19 %	67	12 %
	Above 50000	33	11 %	30	12 %	63	11 %

Results and Analysis

I Demographic analysis

A total of 550 respondents constitutes our sample size, of which 300 are from Delhi city and 250 from Mumbai. The respondents represent a heterogeneous combination of gender, age, qualification, and income. A brief description of the same is as follows: -

Table: Gender Classification

Gender	Delhi Respondents (300)		Mumbai Respondents (250)		Total (550)	
	No.	%	No.	%	No.	%
Males	168	56 %	132	53 %	300	55 %
Females	132	44 %	118	47 %	250	45 %

The above table shows that of the total respondents 55 % are males and 45 % females. Though the proportion of male response is slightly higher in both the cities, but the representation can fairly be assumed to be reasonably equal.

Table: Age classification

Age	Delhi Respondents (300)		Mumbai Respondents (250)		Total (550)	
	No.	%	No.	%	No.	%
Below 20 years (teenagers)	79	26 %	44	18 %	123	22 %
20-30 Years (youth)	167	56 %	151	60 %	318	58 %
30-40 Years (young adults)	40	13 %	39	16 %	79	14 %
Above 40 Years (adults)	14	5 %	16	6 %	30	6 %

Gender Split

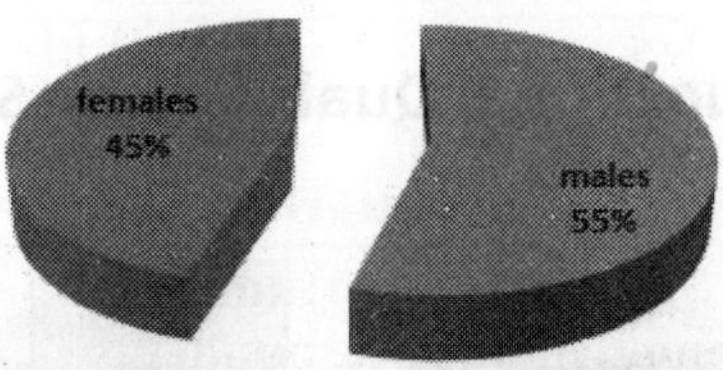

The table depicts the age classification and in both the cities. The youth represented in the age bracket of 20-30 years is the highest at 58 % and of the total 94 % is represented by the young generation.

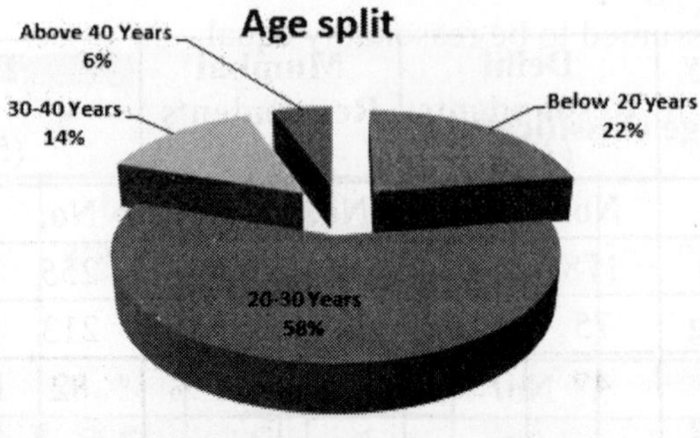

Table: Educational Qualification classification

Educl. Qualification	Delhi Respondents (300)		Mumbai Respondents (250)		Total (550)	
	No.	%	No.	%	No.	%
Graduates	102	34 %	64	26 %	167	34 %
Postgraduates	125	41 %	106	43 %	231	46 %
Others	73	25 %	25	32 %	98	20 %

The educational qualification among the respondents from the two cities is quite high with 46 % post graduates and others represented professionals, Phd. and diploma holders.

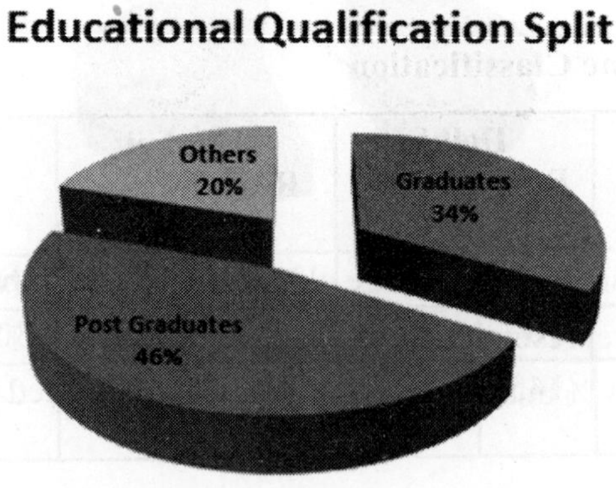

Table: Category Classification

Category	Delhi Respondents (300)		Mumbai Respondents (250)		Total (550)	
	No.	%	No.	%	No.	%
Student	178	60 %	77	31 %	255	46 %
Working	75	25 %	138	55 %	213	39 %
Not Working	47	15 %	35	14 %	82	15 %

As can be seen above from the table the student category is the largest constituting 46 %, 39 % of the respondents are working. The non-working category constitutes just about 15%.

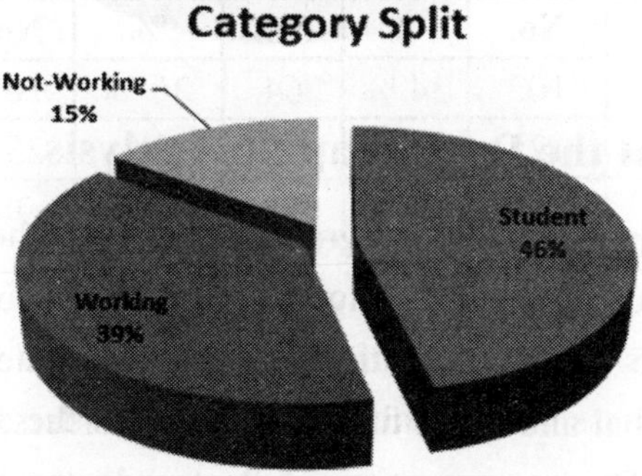

Table: Income Classification

Income (In Rs.)	Delhi Respondents (300)		Mumbai Respondents (250)		Total (550)	
	No.	%	No.	%	No.	%
None	102	34 %	72	29 %	174	32 %
10000-30000	145	48 %	101	40 %	246	45 %

30000-50000	20	7 %	47	19 %	67	12 %
Above 50000	33	11 %	30	12 %	63	11 %

From the income table 67 % of the respondents are earning with income ranging between 10,000-above 50,000.

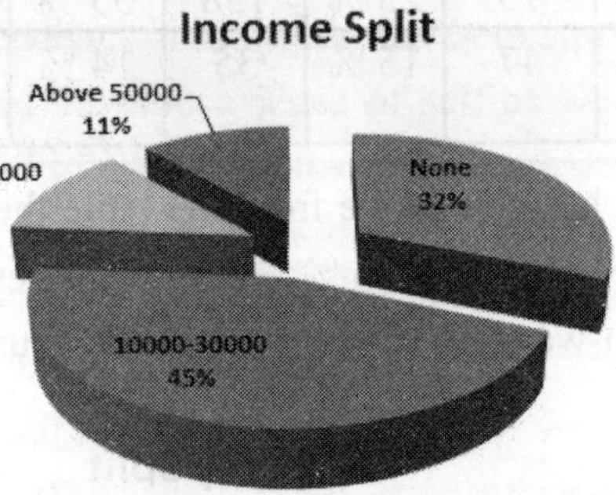

Summary of the Demographic Analysis

An insight into the demographic details of the respondents from the two cities reveals a high concentration of males (55 %) to females (45 %). 94 % of the total is below 40 years with 60 % from Mumbai and 56 % from Delhi within the age bracket of 20-30 years. The concentration of Postgraduates from both the places is high. An important difference was found for the category classification wherein 60 % represented the student category in Delhi and 55 % working class in Mumbai. In all 68 % of our youth respondents are earning.

II Frequency Analysis

To understand further about the use, membership, type, time spent and information revealed in social networking sites frequency analysis was conducted. The results are as follows:

Table: Membership in Social Networking Sites

Member of SNS	Delhi Respondents (300)		Mumbai Respondents (250)		Total (550)	
	No.	%	No.	%	No.	%
Yes	292	97 %	240	96 %	530	96 %
No	8	3 %	10	4 %	20	4 %

Table:

	Delhi		Mumbai		Total	
	Yes	No	Yes	No	Yes	No
Males	164	4	132	0	296	4
Females	128	4	108	10	236	14
Total	**292**	**8**	**240**	**10**	**532**	**18**

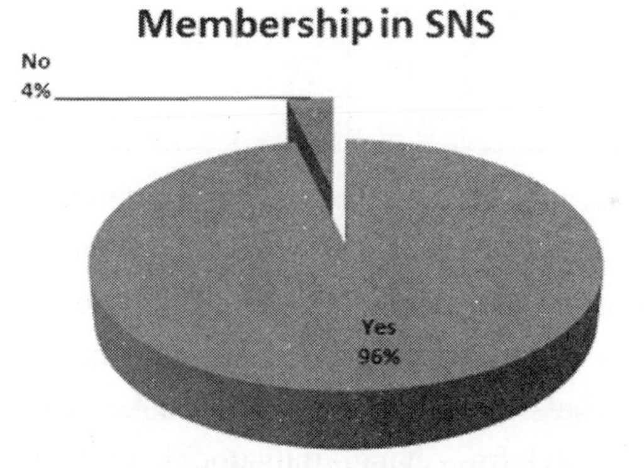

From the pie diagram above a remarkable 96% of our sample was member of one or more social networking sites which clearly makes a strong statement "being a member in one or more social networking sites is a status quo" among Indian youth. Among them 56 % were males and 44 % females. Of those who were not member of any SNS the reasons identified were:

Do not have regular computer access- 78 %

Do not have time- 12 %

Not interested – 7 %

Not aware of any SNS- 3 %

Table: Social Networking sites used

Name of the SNS used	Delhi Respondents		Mumbai Respondents		Total	
	No.	%	No.	%	No.	%
Flikr	52	18 %	24	10 %	76	14 %
Face Book	254	87 %	226	94 %	480	90 %
Twitter	88	30 %	108	45 %	196	37 %
Orkut	44	15 %	43	18 %	87	16 %
Linkidin	102	35 %	110	46 %	212	40 %
My Space	6	2 %	10	4 %	16	3 %
Hi 5	18	6 %	12	5 %	30	6 %
Whats up	204	70 %	204	85 %	408	77 %
Any other	9	3 %	7	3 %	16	3 %

There was an overlapping pattern in the membership of social networking sites where 90 % of the respondents use FB and 77 % WhatsApp. More specifically 33% and 30 % respectively from the two cities were exclusive members of Facebook and 26 % and 27 % in WhatsApp. Any others included Adda, Blogspot.com, WAYN, Hi5, Stylefm, Ning, Indyarocks, ,Netlog, Friendster, ebuddy and Vampirefreaks.

The awareness level in terms of the memberships in SNS and over different types of sites does not differ across the two cities. Facebook and WhatsApp were identified as the most popular among the Indian youth. Thus, our Null hypothesis ‘There is no difference in the Awareness level across the two cities’ is very much accepted.

The results for the same are graphically displayed in the bar chart.

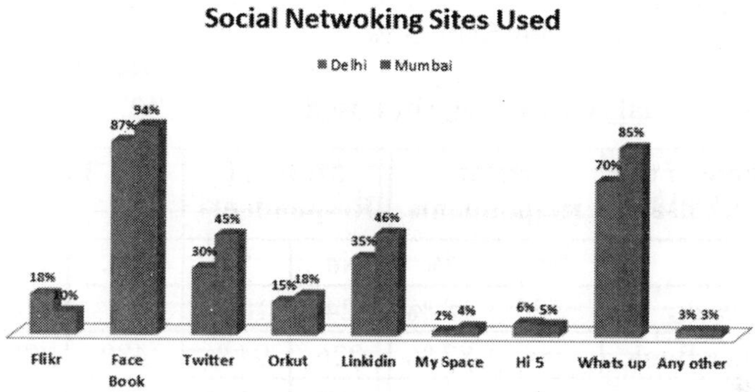

Table: Time spent on the SNS

Number of Hrs. (in a week)	Delhi Respondents (292)		Mumbai Respondents (240))		Total	
	No.	**%**	**No.**	**%**	**No.**	**%**
0 – 5 Hrs	125	42 %	4	2 %	129	24 %
6 – 10 Hrs	42	14 %	75	31 %	117	22 %
11 – 20 Hrs	51	17 %	80	33 %	131	25 %
21 – 30 Hrs	25	9 %	59	25 %	84	16 %
31 – 40 Hrs	15	6 %	22	9 %	37	7 %
More than 40 hrs	34	12 %	-	-	34	6 %

Time spent on the SNS in response to the number of hours in a week spent on internet, the table describes 42 % respondents of Delhi spent just about 0-5 hours in comparison to Mumbai respondents where 33% spent 11-20 hrs. Further the table below shows the time spent by males and females separately in the two cities:

Table:

Number of Hrs. (in a week)	Delhi Respondents (292)		Mumbai Respondents (240))	
	Males	Females	Males	Females
0 – 5 Hrs	69	56	0	11
6 – 10 Hrs	23	19	54	19
11 – 20 Hrs	31	20	44	24
21 – 30 Hrs	18	7	24	40
31 – 40 Hrs	6	9	6	16
More than 40 hrs	17	17	2	0
Total	**164**	**128**	**130**	**110**

The above table depicts the time spent by males and females in two cities on the SNS. 43 % males and 44 % females in Delhi spend 0-5 hrs in a week in comparison to 44 % males spending 6 -10 hrs and 34 % females spending 21- 30 hrs in a week. Further the average time spent is 13.9 hrs in Delhi both for males and females while it is 15.4 hrs for males and 20.4 hrs for females in Mumbai city. Mumbai female youth spends more hours on the SNS than the Delhi youth. Our hypothesis 'There is no difference in the usage of SNS across the two cities' was not supported.

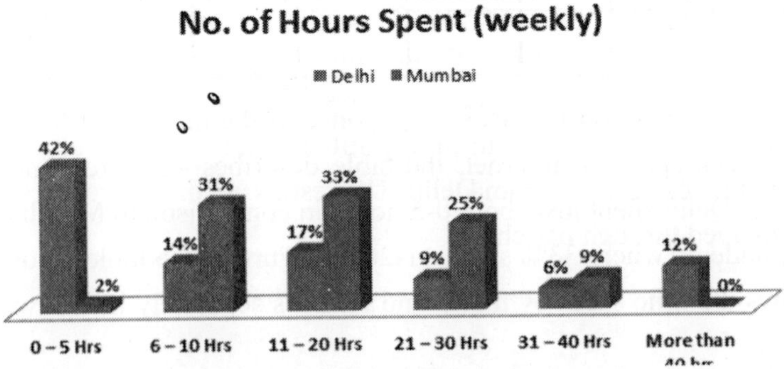

Table: Information Revealed on SNS

Profile information	Delhi Respondents (292)		Mumbai Respondents (240))		Total	
	No.	%	No.	%	No.	%
Name / Identity	254	87 %	216	92 %	470	88 %
Email	181	62 %	137	57 %	318	60 %
Hometown/ City	199	68 %	168	70 %	367	69%
IM address	61	21 %	84	35 %	145	27 %
Mobile No.	102	35 %	96	40 %	198	37 %
Photos	251	86 %	228	95 %	479	90 %
Relation-ship status	88	30 %	96	40 %	184	35 %
Date of Birth	199	68 %	173	72 %	372	70 %
Place of work	140	48 %	72	30 %	212	40 %
Interests/ likes	158	54 %	132	55 %	290	55 %
Any other	3	1 %		-	3	0.4 %

Comparative tables on the information revealed by the respondents of the two cities shows Mumbai respondents are more open and upfront in giving information about themselves than the respondents from Delhi. The results are diagrammatically displayed through bar chart.

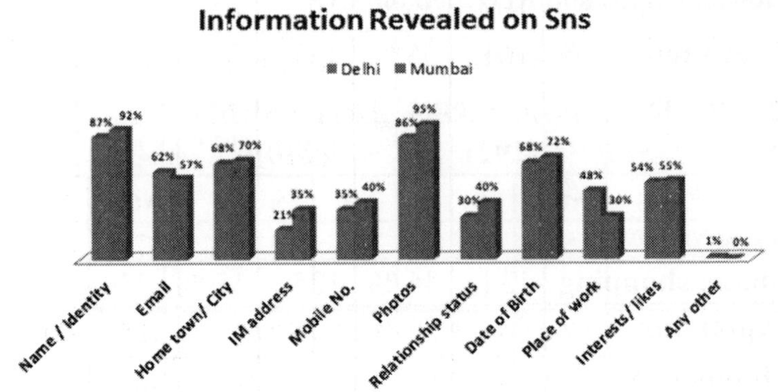

Table: Purpose/ uses of SNS

Purposes/ Aims	Delhi Respon-dents (292)		Mumbai Respon-dents (240)		Total	
	No.	%	No.	%	No.	%
Chatting & Messaging	99	34 %	96	40 %	195	37%
Networking/ developing contacts	242	83 %	204	85 %	446	84 %
Sharing/ uploading snaps	190	65 %	134	56 %	324	61 %
Checking status of others	152	52 %	110	46 %	262	49 %
Updating your status	117	40 %	115	48 %	232	44 %
Seeking & giving information	161	55 %	142	59 %	303	57 %

Entertainment	102	35 %	101	42 %	203	38 %
Education & knowledge	161	55 %	137	57 %	298	56 %
Job opportunities & employment	99	34 %	113	47 %	212	40 %
Online shopping	134	46 %	125	52 %	259	49 %
Expressing opinions on different issues	88	30 %	101	42 %	189	36 %

On the purposes and reasons for registering on sns, a vast majority from both the cities use it for networking and developing contacts (84 %). Re-establishing with old colleagues and friends and making new friends were the reasons cited. 57 % use it for sharing information and 56 % for education and knowledge sharing. An upcoming area of 0nlie shopping is also gaining momentum. Though it so more popular among Mumbai respondents (52 %) in comparison to Delhi respondents (46 %). In response to expressing opinions on different issues, Youth from Mumbai seemed more expressive in giving online opinions than the Delhi youths.

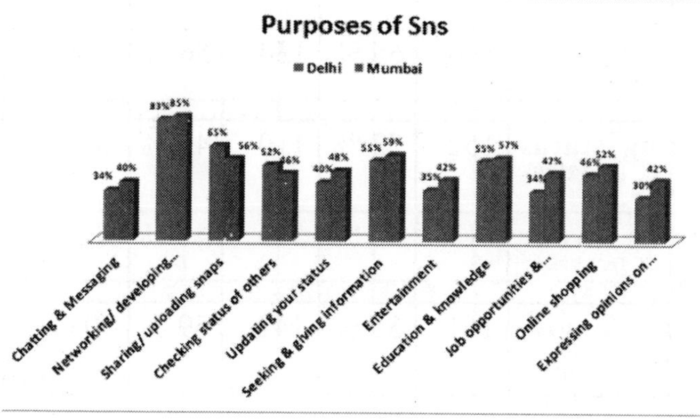

Summary of Frequency Analysis

96 % of the youth have an account over SNS. Facebook is the most popular among both the cities followed by WhatsApp. The average time spent on SNS in Mumbai is higher than Delhi. Further, females spend more hours than their male counterparts (almost about 3 hours per day). In terms of the reasons/ purposes of SNS, a sizable majority 84 % use it for chatting and networking. 56 % of the time spent is on enhancing education and knowledge. An important revelation emerged in the context of online shopping and expressing opinions over issues of social and political concerns wherein both are gaining momentum over the social sites.

III Descriptive Analysis

Table: Impact and influence of SNS on the lifestyles of Indian Youth

S. No.	State-ments	Delhi Respondents (N = 292)		Mumbai Respondents (N = 240))		Total (N = 532)	
		Mean	S. D	Mean	S. D	Mean	S. D
1.	Being part of SNS is important and significant	3.38	.521`	3.42	.495	3.39	.509
2.	Profiles & updates reflect status & personality	3.04	.634	3.29	.417	3.17	.559
3.	SNS Influe-nces life-styles w.r.t						

a.	Personal growth/ devt.	2.92	1.33	3.13	.597	3.03	1.07
b.	Professional growth	2.82	.702	2.88	.555	2.85	.640
c.	Relationships	2.75	.660	2.50	.622	2.64	.655
d.	Education & Know-ledge	3.14	.806	3.29	.661	3.22	.772
e.	Health & Fitness	2.39	.848	2.66	.873	2.51	.870
		3.23	.284	3.36	.203		

The above table describes the mean score of the youth on the impact and influence of SNS on their lifestyles. For the youth of Mumbai city being part of sns today is important (mean = 3.42) as also the updates reflect their status and personality (mean = 3.29) in comparison to the youth of Delhi. A comparison to all the dimensions of lifestyles respondents for both the cities regard education and knowledge (mean = 3.29 in Mumbai and mean =3.14 in Delhi) to be the most influenced. The overall average score (mean = 3.30) for the two cities is high ranging between agree to strongly agree which is indicative of the fact that for the Indian youth today.

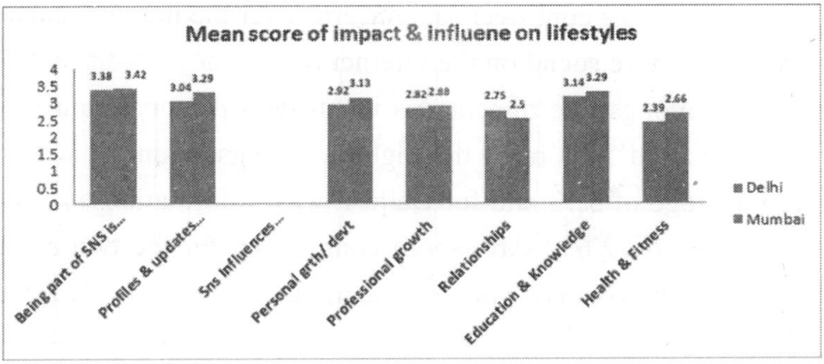

Table: Level of Trust on the SNS

S. No.	Statements	Delhi Respon-dents (N = 292)		Mumbai Respon-dents (N = 240)		Total (N = 532)	
		Mean	**S. D**	**Mean**	**S. D**	**Mean**	**S. D**
1.	Privacy of my information is protected on the sns	2.65	.729	2.96	.551	2.79	.675
2.	Trust on SNS that they will not misuse personal details	2.61	.803	3.03	.641	2.82	.764
3.	Information collected from sns is true	2.51	.753	3.47	.500	3.00	.807
		2.58	.425	3.15	.314		

The above table depicts the descriptive scores of the level of trust and privacy among the respondents of the two cities. Privacy is one of the most controversial concerns over the internet and as we become more social on the internet our privacy becomes vulnerable. Amongst the dimensions identified, 'personal data will not be misused' was rated the highest amongst Mumbai with a mean average of 3.13 and for Delhi it was 'information on SNS is true', mean= 2.65. An overall comparison for the two cities depicts that the youth of Mumbai had more trust and confidence in sharing and using SNS as their responses ranged between agree-strongly agree in contrast to Delhi youth where the responses ranged between agree to disagree.

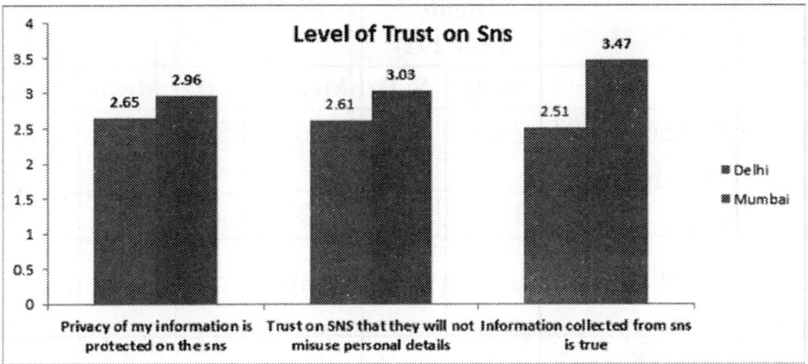

Table: Social Issues discussed and its likely impact

S. No.	Statements	Delhi Respon-dents (N = 292)		Mumbai Respon-dents (N = 240)		Total (N = 532)	
		Mean	S. D	Mean	S. D	Mean	S. D
1.	SNS are Important platform for discussing social-eco-nomic issues	3.20	.565	3.01	.596	3.11	.579
2.	Political concerns have gained momentum through SNS.	3.41	.519	3.48	.675	3.44	.594

3.	New brand identity to Modi & Kejriwal in the recent Lok Sabha elections	3.38	.670	3.32	.357	3.35	.652
		3.33	.552	3.27	.476		

As can be inferred from the table above on the social issues discussed, they have gained momentum in the recent past. The mean scores for the respondents in both cities range between 3.01-3.48 with lo S. D. This is indicative of the fact that the youth today agrees that social issues, political concerns, and opinions on elections are widely being discussed on the SNS and believe that they help in building brand identities to the representatives.

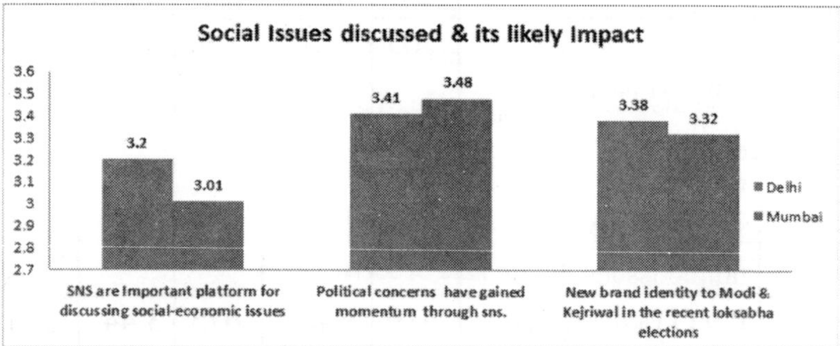

Table: Future Role of social media

S. No.	Statements	Delhi Respon-dents (N = 292)		Mumbai Respon-dents (N = 240)		Total (N = 532)	
		Mean	S. D	Mean	S. D	Mean	S. D

1.	Groups/ communities on the SNS will advance greater awareness in the future.	3.37	.517	3.27	.557	3.42	.537
2.	Future social media will have an important role for national development	3.41	.616	3.33	.627	3.37	.621
		3.39	.543	3.30	.467		

The above table depicts the mean scores of the youth regarding the future role of social media. As can be inferred from the table the overall mean score of Delhi is 3.39 as against Mumbai at 3.30. Though the Sns have been a recent development on internet but has fast gained momentum. The Indian youth is highly assertive to the role of social media for nation development (mean =3.37) and also on the future role of sns in creating greater awareness (mean = 3.42).

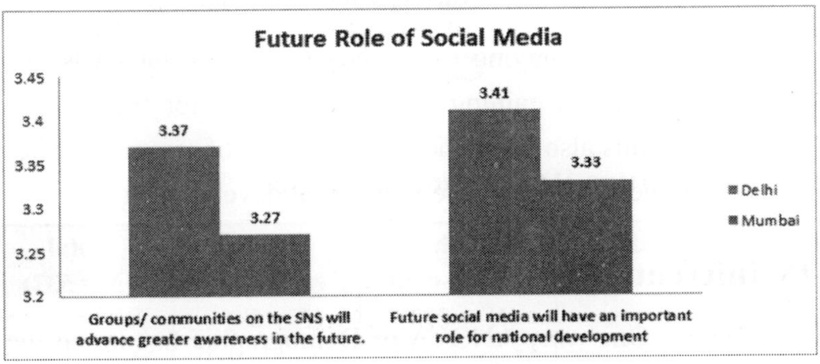

Summary of Demographic Analysis

The results of the above descriptive analysis are summarized as under:

- Being part of SNS is important for the youth today as they reflect the status and lifestyles. They identify education and knowledge followed by personal growth and development to be the most influenced. This could be attributed to the fact that the majority of our respondents (about 46 %) were students.
- For the level of trust on the sites, Mumbai youth seemed to be more open in giving and sharing information in comparison to Delhi youth. Though overall they are not too sure of the privacy of their personal details but agree to the authenticity of the information obtained through the sns.
- There is a consensus among the Indian youth that SNS are important platforms for discussing issues, though Delhi youth are more upfront for socio-economic issues whereas Mumbai youth are more for political concerns, but both agree to the new brand identity created for Narender Modi and Arvind Kejriwal through social media.
- There is no denying to the fact that social media is fast emerging and gaining a significant role for the society, our results also bring the same in terms of creating greater awareness and their role in national development

IV Inferential Analysis

Table: One- way ANOVA of Demographic factors on the lifestyles of Indian Youth

Demographic Factors		Sum of Squares	D.F	Mean Square	F Score	Sig.
Age	Between Groups	.545	2	.182	2.561	.014
	Within Groups	37.09	530	.011		
	Total	37.64	532			
Gender	Between Groups	.489	2	.489	6.907	.009
	Within Groups	37.14	530	.071		
	Total	37.63	532			
Education	Between Groups	.146	2	.073	1.02	.362
	Within Groups	37.49	530	.072		
	Total	37.64	532			
Category	Between Groups	.494	2	.247	1.49	.642
	Within Groups	37.14	530	.071		
	Total	37.64	532			
Income	Between Groups	.811	2	.270	**3.839**	.010
	Within Groups	36.75	530	.070		
	Total	37.56	532			

The ANOVA results above reveal statistically significant difference in the group means of demographic factors of age groups, gender, and income categories. The impact and influence of sns is seen to be varying among different age groups, a further Post Hoc test (Tukey's) revealed significant differences by the age- group

'20-30 years'. Similarly for income category the differences were more significant for'10,000-30,000' category. Our null hypothesis 'Social networking sites do not have any impact and influence on the lifestyles of Indian youth w.r. t the demographic factors' was thus partially accepted

Table: T-test for impact and influence

	Statement	Delhi		Mumbai		t score	D.F	Sig.	Result
		Mean	S.D	Mean	S.D				
1.	Being Part of Sns is significant in today's scenario.	3.38	.521	3.42	.495	.939	530	.348	NS
2.	My Profiles & updates reflect status & personality.	3.04	.634	3.29	.417	4.73*	530	.000	S
3.	SNS have important influence on my life-styles w.r t								
a	Personal grth & devt.	2.92	.533	3.13	.597	2.16	530	.231	NS
b	Professional Growth	2.82	.702	2.88	.555	1.13	530	.258	NS
c	Relationships	2.75	.650	2.50	.622	4.48*	530	.000	S
d	Education & Knowledge	3.14	.806	3.29	.661	1.13	530	..634	NS
e	Health & Fitness	2.39	.848	2.66	.873	3.63*	530	.000	S
	Overall	3.23	.284	3.36	.203	2.42*	530	.000	S

N= 532, *p<.05

As can be observed from the table above significant differences were observed between the two cities w.r.t the responses on the impact and influence of SNS on their lifestyles. The youth in Mumbai were more concerned about their profiles and updates as it reflected their status and personality (mean: 3.29, S.D =.417 in Mumbai in comparison of mean: 3.04, S.D =.634 In Delhi).

More specifically the differenced were significant for relationships, and Health & Fitness.

Table: T-test for Privacy and Trust

	Statement	Delhi		Mumbai		t score	D.F	Sig.	Result
		Mean	S. D	Mean	S. D				
1.	Privacy of my personal information is protected on SNS.	2.65	.729	2.96	.551	5.84*	530	.000	S
2.	SNS will not use my personal information for any other purpose.	2.61	.803	3.03	.641	6.591*	530	.000	S
3.	Information collected through SNS is correct	2.51	.753	3.47	.500	16.81*	530	.000	S
	Overall	2.58	.425	3.15	.314	17.24*	530	.000	S

N= 532, *p<.05

The responses for privacy and trust on the SNS for the two cities also differed significantly as can be observed from the table above. The respondents in Mumbai were surer on the information collected through networking sites and the privacy of their personal information on these sites than the respondents in Delhi. Thus, the null hypothesis framed 'There is no difference in responses from the two cities on the issues of privacy and trust on Sns' was rejected as marked differences emerged across the cities on the above concerns.

Table: T-test for Knowledge on social issues

S. No.	Statement	Delhi		Mumbai		t score	D.F	Sig.	Re sult
		Mean	S. D	Mean	S. D				
1.	SNS are relevant platforms to discuss socio-economic issues.	3.20	.565	3.01	.596	1.11	530	.269	NS
2.	Recent political concerns / issues in our country have gained momentum through SNS.	3.41	.519	3.48	.675	1.33	530	.185	NS
3.	New brand identities due to social media to Narender Modi and Arvind Kejriwal	3.38	.670	3.32	.357	1.01	530	.315	NS
	Overall	3.26	.366	3.25	.357	.514	530	.607	NS

N= 532, *p<.05

The independent t-test conducted above to find the difference if any for knowledge and awareness on social issues among the two cities was not found to be significant. It is indicative of the fact that the youth across India today is very much concerned on the socio-economic issues and political concerns and find SNS as a strong medium to express their opinions and raise voice. The null hypothesis for the same 'There is lack of knowledge on the social networking sites on the social issues discussed' was not supported as respondents from both cities expressed fair concerns on the same as reflected by high mean score and the differences across was not found to be statistically significant.

Table: T-test for Future role of SNS

S. No.	Statement	Delhi		Mumbai		t score	D.F	Sig.	Re-sult
		Mean	S. D	Mean	S. D				
1.	Groups/ communities on the SNS will advance greater awareness in the future.	3.37	.517	3.27	.557	2.01	530	.650	NS
2.	Future social media will have an important role for national development	3.41	.616	3.33	.627	1.43	530	.554	NS
	Overall	3.39	3.89	3.30	.436	1.47	530	.614	NS

N= 532, *p<.05

As can be inferred from the table above for the differences among Delhi and Mumbai respondents for the upcoming role of social media, t-test does not specify statistically significant results (t= 1.47, p= .614). A high mean score for the two aspects with a narrow range of dispersion for the two cities indicates that youth today believe that the groups/ communities on the sns will create better and greater awareness and also have an important role in the nation development. Our hypothesis' Youth participation is not significant in social development and nation building' was thus not supported by the results.

Summary of Inferential Analysis

- Age, Gender, and Income were identified as distinguishing demographic criterions influencing lifestyles of Indian youth through sns.
- A comparative analysis of the two cities highlighted:
- Statistically significant differences in terms of the impact and influence of the networking. More peculiar is the difference of sharing and disclosing profiles and updates, here Mumbai youth seemed to be more casual and open and Delhi youth was reluctant and cautious. Also, the impact on the relationships as found to be of concern across the two cities.
- Another highlighting difference was w.r.t to the concern of privacy issues wherein again significant difference was found. The respondents from Mumbai expressed more confidence and Delhi respondents more apprehensiveness to the trust and privacy concerns over sns.
- No statistical differences were found for the 'knowledge on social issues' and the 'future role of social media' across cities. This is an indication that socio-economic issues and political concerns are gaining momentum and are being constructively used to build new brand identities.

There is no denying the fast-emerging role of social media for knowledge, understanding and nation development. It has grown from 'going viral' to creating 'meaningful engagements.

CHAPTER XIII

Conclusion And Discussions

The main aim of our study was to explore the attitude of the Indian youth across the country and use of new communications phenomenon, internet, and Social Networking Sites. Due to financial constraints, as is inevitable in vast studies of such type we could collect data only from two cities – Delhi and Mumbai. Research undertaken on 550 youths from different private and government institutions brought out many interesting insights. Social networking sites are very important for the social development of students as they can share and develop their opinion on the information provided by social capitals, certainly it is used to frame people's comments. In India, where the internet penetration is excellent as the educational institution is well equipped with new media tools and thus, the SNS's like Facebook, Tweeter, E-Mail user has a set of loyal visitors today (Turkle, S. 1995). The study revealed that for many users online social networking has become a hobby, and for a few it has become a bit of a confidence building instrument. Several users simply said that there is no life without SNS's. There is no doubt this social media has brought a massive change in Indian youth especially in their lifestyle and nation building. Growing popularity of E-commerce, E-business in fashion and lifestyle product to consumer items to Anna movement to current Loksabha and assembly election has been fighting with social media.

There is no denying to the fact that social media is being extensively and widely used medium of communication and staying connected. Apart from that it is also evolving as a mass mobilisation medium for expressing and creating significant concerns on our socio-political issues. Growing from 'going viral' to creating 'meaningful engagements' has much repercussion on positive implication for our society and nation development.

The recent research show that over the past decade the various social networking sites have created a phenomenon with their popularity among the masses. Twitter and Facebook emerged as the two most popular websites creating new ways of communicating with family and friends and also grooming the person and influencing his individual concept. These computer mediated sites provide the layman with the most innovative mode of communication thus making it faster and easier to communicate and share stories all over the world. These SNS make the contact of reach limitless. Based on a survey the findings show that enjoyment followed by the number of active peers and the usefulness of the various media as the respective order of perceived benefits from the SNS. The study also laid down the factors affecting both men and women leading to increasing use of the social media. The findings suggested that gender differences produced different types of influences. The number of peers was proven to be a stronger influence on women while it showed that this had absolutely no effect on enjoyment for the men. It has become necessary as well as a trend to stay connected in the information age. It can also not be denied that social networking sites have now become the part and parcel of the industries and workforce. But with increased use of the SNS also comes the responsibility of using the sites and the technology with utmost care. One must be vigilant about what one is posting and sharing online. The boundaries of the cyber conduct must be followed thus preventing various online cybercrimes.

On an average user checks their Facebook and other social media apps at least 5-10 times in a day spending all most a 24 hour in a week in social media to update their information. Users said that keeping contact with distant friends and reaching many social contacts at same time were the key aspects of social networking websites appeals. Some of the youth users conform that spending hours looking on the profile, posting comments, managing their own profile, and learning by interaction with valuable information defiantly increases their confidence. Thus, some of the conclusions drawn:

- Being part of SNS is important for the youth today as they reflect the status and lifestyles. They identify education and knowledge followed by personal growth and development to be the most influenced. This could be attributed to the fact that majority of our respondents (about 46 %) were students.
- For the level of trust on the sites, Mumbai youth seemed to be more open in giving and sharing information in comparison to Delhi youth. Though overall they are not too sure of the privacy of their personal details but agree to the authenticity of the information obtained through the sns.
- There is a consensus among the Indian youth that sns are important platforms for discussing issues, though Delhi youth are more upfront for socio-economic issues whereas Mumbai youth are more for political concerns, but both agree to the new brand identity created for Narender Modi and Arvind Kejriwal through social media.

- Age, Gender, and Income were identified as distinguishing demographic criterions influencing lifestyles of Indian youth through SNS.
- A comparative analysis of the two cities highlighted:

✦ Statistically significant differences in terms of the impact and influence of the networking. More peculiar is the difference of sharing and disclosing profiles and updates, here Mumbai youth seemed to be more casual and open and Delhi youth was reluctant and cautious. Also, the impact on the relationships as found to be of concern across the two cities.

✦ Another highlighting difference was w.r.t to the concern of privacy issues wherein again significant difference was found. The respondents from Mumbai expressed more confidence and Delhi respondents more apprehensiveness to the trust and privacy concerns over sns.

✦ No statistical differences were found for the 'knowledge on social issues' and the 'future role of social media' across cities. This is an indication that socio-economic issues and political concerns are gaining momentum and are being constructively used to build new brand identities.

After going into the details of each aspect of the brilliant phenomenon called 'social media', the reader may have developed a better knowledge of varying facets of it. The way it had impacted the lives of people, no other revolution would have done so far. Taking into consideration all the impacts and developments, I hope this report may prove useful to the reader.

References

CHAPTER I

An overview of the social media

- Byrne, D. N. (2008). The future of (the)'race': Identity, discourse and the rise of computer-mediated public spheres. MacArthur Foundation Book Series on Digital Learning: Race and Ethnicity Volume, 15-38.
- Chen, R. (2013). Living a private life in public social networks: An exploration of member self-disclosure. Decision Support Systems, 55(3), 661-668.
- Chen, R. (2013). Member use of social networking sites—an empirical examination. Decision Support Systems, 54(3), 1219-1227.
- Choi, S. M., Kim, Y., Sung, Y., & Sohn, D. (2011). Bridging or Bonding? A cross-cultural study of social relationships in social networking sites. Information, Communication & Society, 14(1), 107-129.
- Kaigo, M., & Tkach-Kawasaki, L. (2012). Social Media Usage for Civil Society in Japanese Municipalities. CeDEM Asia 2012, 59.
- Lenhart, A., & Madden, M. (2007). Social networking websites and teens: An overview (p. 10). Pew/Internet.

- Lin, C. Y. (2008, March). Educational Blogs: From Social Issues to Blogs' Applications and Implications in Teacher Education Programs. In Society for Information Technology & Teacher Education International Conference (Vol. 2008, No. 1, pp. 2701-2706).
- Mayfield, A. (2008). What is social media.
- Pérez-Sabater, C. (2012). The linguistics of social networking: A study of writing conventions on Facebook. Linguistik online, 56(6/12), 82.
- Smith, T. (2009). The social media revolution. International journal of market research, 51(4), 559-561.
- http://www.edutopia.org/blog social- media-five-key-concepts-stacey-goodman
- http://webtrends.about.com/od/web20/a/social-media.htm
- http://webcomm.tufts.edu/social-media-overview13/
- http://www.webopedia.com/TERM/S/social_networking_site.html
- https://www.nibusinessinfo.co.uk/content/ advantages-and-disadvantages-using-social-media
- http://au.professionals.reachout.com/ benefits-of-internet-and-social-media

CHAPTER II

Social Media concept and definition

- Brinlee D. (2007). Does Internet Advertising Work, http:// www.askdeb.com /internet/advertising.

- Chaffey D (2003). Internet Marketing, Strategy, Implementation and Practise. 2 edition, Pearson Education Limited, pp. 115-186.
- C. Lampe, N. Ellison, and C. Steinfield, "A Face(book) in the Crowd: Social Searching vs. Social Browsing," Proc. 20th Anniv. Conf. on Comput. Supported Cooperative Work (CSCW '06) (Banff, Alberta, Can., 2006), pp. 167–170.
- Adamic, L., & Adar, E. (2005). How to search a social network. Social Networks, 27(3), 187-203.
- Adamic, L., Buyukkokten, O., & Adar, E. (2003). A social network caught in the web. First Monday, 8(6).
- Boyd, D. M., & Ellison, N. B. (2010). Social network sites: definition, history, and scholarship. Engineering Management Review, IEEE, 38(3), 16-31.
- Dietrich, B. J. Are Online Social Networks Communities?: A Social Network Analysis of Facebook.
- Ellison, N. B. (2007). Social network sites: Definition, history, and scholarship. Journal of Computer□Mediated Communication, 13(1), 210-230.
- Lampe, C., Ellison, N., & Steinfield, C. (2006, November). A Face (book) in the crowd: Social searching vs. social browsing. In Proceedings of the 2006 20th anniversary conference on Computer supported cooperative work (pp. 167-170). ACM.

CHAPTER III

History and evolution of social media

- Backstrom, L., Huttenlocher, D., Kleinberg, J., & Lan, X. (2006). Group formation in large social networks: Membership, growth, and evolution. Proceedings of 12th International Conference on Knowledge Discovery in Data Mining (pp. 44–54). New York: ACM Press.
- Cassidy, J. (2006). Me media: How hanging out on the Internet became big business. The New Yorker, 82(13), 50.
- Ghosh, S., & Ganguly, N. (2014). Structure and Evolution of Online Social Networks. In Social Networking (pp. 23-44). Springer International Publishing.
- Kumar, R., Novak, J., & Tomkins, A. (2010). Structure and evolution of online social networks. In Link mining: models, algorithms, and applications (pp. 337-357). Springer New York.
- Leskovec, J., Backstrom, L., Kumar, R., & Tomkins, A. (2008, August). n Proceedings of the 14th ACM SIGKDD international conference on Knowledge discovery and data mining (pp. 462-470). ACM.
- Merchant, G. (2012). Unravelling the social network: theory and research. Learning, Media and Technology, 37(1), 4-19.
- Mislove, A., Marcon, M., Gummadi, K. P., Druschel, P., & Bhattacharjee, B. (2007, October). Measurement and analysis of online social networks. In Proceedings of the 7th ACM SIGCOMM conference on Internet measurement (pp. 29-42). ACM.

CHAPTER IV
Type of Social Media

- Bruns, A. (2008). Blogs, Wikipedia, Second Life, and beyond: From production to produsage (Vol. 45). Peter Lang.
- Kaplan, A. M., & Haenlein, M. (2010). Users of the world, unite! The challenges and opportunities of Social Media. Business horizons, 53(1), 59-68.
- Kaplan, A. M., & Haenlein, M. (2011). The early bird catches the news: Nine things you should know about micro-blogging. Business Horizons, 54(2), 105-113.
- Katz, J. E., & Rice, R. E. (2002). Social consequences of Internet use: Access, involvement, and interaction (pp. 1-463). Cambridge, MA: MIT press.
- Kietzmann, J. H., Hermkens, K., McCarthy, I. P., & Silvestre, B. S. (2011). Social media? Get serious! Understanding the functional building blocks of social media. Business horizons, 54(3), 241-251.
- Richardson, W. W. H. (2010). Blogs, wikis, podcasts, and other powerful web tools for classrooms. Corwin Press.
- Thelwall, M. (2008). Social networks, gender, and friending: An analysis of MySpace member profiles. Journal of the American Society for Information Science and Technology, 59(8), 1321-1330.

CHAPTER V
Some popular Social Networking Sites

- Boyd, D. (2006). Friends, Friendster, and MySpace top 8: Writing community into being on social network sites.
- Chen, J., Geyer, W., Dugan, C., Muller, M., & Guy, I. (2009, April). Make new friends, but keep the old: recommending people on social networking sites. In Proceedings of the SIGCHI Conference on Human Factors in Computing Systems (pp. 201-210). ACM.
- Hei-Man, T. (2008). An Ethnography of social networks in cyberspace: The Facebook phenomenon. The Hong Kong Anthropologist, 2, 53-76.
- Kwak, H., Lee, C., Park, H., & Moon, S. (2010, April). What is Twitter, a social network or a news media? In Proceedings of the 19th international conference on the World Wide Web (pp. 591-600). ACM.
- Leskovec, J., Backstrom, L., Kumar, R., & Tomkins, A. (2008, August). Microscopic evolution of social networks. In Proceedings of the 14th ACM SIGKDD international conference on Knowledge discovery and data mining (pp. 462-470). ACM.
- Murray, K. E., & Waller, R. (2007). Social networking goes abroad. International Educator, 16(3), 56-59.
- Rivera, J., Davis, F., Mouloua, M., & Alberti, P. (2010, September). Usability evaluation of two social networking sites. In Proceedings of the Human Factors and Ergonomics Society Annual Meeting (Vol. 54, No. 19, pp. 1421-1424). SAGE Publications.

- Russell, M. A. (2013). Mining the Social Web: Data Mining Facebook, Twitter, LinkedIn, Google+, GitHub, and More. " O'Reilly Media, Inc.".
- Skeels, M. M., & Grudin, J. (2009, May). When social networks cross boundaries: a case study of workplace use of Facebook and LinkedIn. In Proceedings of the ACM 2009 international conference on supporting group work (pp. 95-104). ACM.
- Spertus, E., Sahami, M., & Buyukkokten, O. (2005, August). Evaluating similarity measures: a large-scale study in the orkut social network. In Proceedings of the eleventh ACM SIGKDD international conference on Knowledge discovery in data mining (pp. 678-684). ACM.

CHAPTER VI

Growing popularity of social media: why is Social Media a Hit?

- Arnett, J. J. (2000). Emerging adulthood: A theory of development from the late teens through the twenties. American psychologist, 55(5), 469.
- Baker, L. R., & Oswald, D. L. (2010). Shyness and online social networking services. Journal of Social and Personal Relationships, 27(7), 873-889.
- Baym, N. K., Zhang, Y. B., & Lin, M. C. (2004). Social Interactions Across Media Interpersonal Communication on the Internet, Telephone and Face-to-Face. New Media & Society, 6(3), 299-318.
- Baym, N. K., Zhang, Y. B., Kunkel, A., Ledbetter, A., & Lin, M. C. (2007). Relational quality and media use in

interpersonal relationships. New Media & Society, 9(5), 735-752.

- Correa, T., Hinsley, A. W., & De Zuniga, H. G. (2010). Who interacts on the Web?: The intersection of users' personality and social media use. Computers in Human Behavior, 26(2), 247-253.
- Davis, F. D., Bagozzi, R. P., & Warshaw, P. R. (1992). Extrinsic and intrinsic motivation to use computers in the workplace1. Journal of applied social psychology, 22(14), 1111-1132.
- Hogan, B., & Quan-Haase, A. (2010). Persistence and change in social media. Bulletin of Science, Technology & Society, 30(5), 309-315.
- Jiang, L., Bazarova, N. N., & Hancock, J. T. (2011). The Disclosure–Intimacy Link in Computer□Mediated Communication: An Attributional Extension of the Hyperpersonal Model. Human Communication Research, 37(1), 58-77.
- Kane, G. C., Fichman, R. G., Gallaugher, J., & Glaser, J. (2009). Community relations 2.0. Harvard Business Review, 87(11), 45-50.
- Katz, M. L., & Shapiro, C. (1985). Network externalities, competition, and compatibility. The American economic review, 424-440.
- Kim, J., & Lee, J. E. R. (2011). The Facebook paths to happiness: Effects of the number of Facebook friends and self-presentation on subjective well-being.

Cyberpsychology, Behavior, and Social Networking, 14(6), 359-364.

- Lenhart, A., Purcell, K., Smith, A., & Zickuhr, K. (2010). Social media and young adults. Pew Internet & American Life Project, 3.
- Lin, C. P., & Bhattacherjee, A. (2008). Elucidating individual intention to use interactive information technologies: The role of network externalities. International Journal of Electronic Commerce, 13(1), 85-108.
- Lin, C. P., & Bhattacherjee, A. (2009). Understanding online social support and its antecedents: A socio-cognitive model. The social science journal, 46(4), 724-737.
- Lin, K. Y., & Lu, H. P. (2011). Why people use social networking sites: An empirical study integrating network externalities and motivation theory. Computers in Human Behavior, 27(3), 1152-1161.
- Liu, X., & LaRose, R. (2008). Does using the Internet make people more satisfied with their lives? The effects of the Internet on college students' school life satisfaction. CyberPsychology & Behavior, 11(3), 310-320.
- Pae, J. H., & Hyun, J. S. (2002). The impact of technology advancement strategies on consumers' patronage decisions. Journal of Product Innovation Management, 19(5), 375-383.
- Pempek, T. A., Yermolayeva, Y. A., & Calvert, S. L. (2009). College students' social networking experiences on Facebook. Journal of Applied Developmental Psychology, 30(3), 227-238.

- Quan-Haase, A., & Young, A. L. (2010). Uses and gratifications of social media: A comparison of Facebook and instant messaging. Bulletin of Science, Technology & Society, 30(5), 350-361.
- Sheldon, P. (2008). STUDENT FAVORITE: FACEBOOK AND MOTIVES FOR ITS USE. Southwestern Mass Communication Journal, 23(2).
- Sponcil, M., & Gitimu, P. (2012). Use of social media by college students: Relationship to communication and self-concept. Journal of Technology Research, 4, 16-28.
- Subrahmanyam, K., Reich, S. M., Waechter, N., & Espinoza, G. (2008). Online and offline social networks: Use of social networking sites by emerging adults. Journal of Applied Developmental Psychology, 29(6), 420-433.
- Tufekci, Z. (2008). Grooming, gossip, Facebook and MySpace: What can we learn about these sites from those who won't assimilate?. Information, Communication & Society, 11(4), 544-564.
- Urista, M. A., Dong, Q., & Day, K. D. (2009). Explaining why young adults use MySpace and Facebook through uses and gratifications theory. Human Communication, 12(2), 215-229.
- West, A., Lewis, J., & Currie, P. (2009). Students' Facebook 'friends': public and private spheres. Journal of youth studies, 12(6), 615-627.

CHAPTER VII

Impact of social media on Lifestyle

- Acquisti, A., & Gross, R. (2006, January). Imagined communities: Awareness, information sharing, and privacy on the Facebook. In Privacy enhancing technologies (pp. 36-58). Springer Berlin Heidelberg.
- Asad, S., Mamun, M. A. A., & Clement, C. K. (2012). The Effect of Social Networking Sites to the Lifestyles of Teachers and Students in Higher Educational Institutions. International Journal of Basic and Applied Sciences, 1(4), 498-510.
- Atkinson, N. L., Saperstein, S. L., & Pleis, J. (2009). Using the internet for health-related activities: findings from a national probability sample. Journal of Medical Internet Research, 11(1).
- Chou, W. Y. S., Hunt, Y. M., Beckjord, E. B., Moser, R. P., & Hesse, B. W. (2009). Social media use in the United States: implications for health communication. Journal of medical Internet research, 11(4).
- Constantinides, E. (2014). Foundations of Social Media Marketing. Procedia-Social and Behavioral Sciences, 148, 40-57.
- Dutta, S. (2010). What's your personal social media strategy? Harvard Business Review, 88(11), 127-130.
- Lenhart, A., Purcell, K., Smith, A., & Zickuhr, K. (2010). Social Media & Mobile Internet Use among Teens and

Young Adults. Millennials. Pew Internet & American Life Project.

- Strater, K., & Richter, H. (2007, July). Examining privacy and disclosure in a social networking community. In Proceedings of the 3rd symposium on Usable privacy and security (pp. 157-158). ACM.
- Valkenburg, P. M., & Peter, J. (2009). Social consequences of the internet for adolescents a decade of research. Current Directions in Psychological Science, 18(1), 1-5.
- Van Eijck, K., & Bargeman, B. (2004). The changing impact of social background on lifestyle: "culturalization" instead of individualization? Poetics, 32(6), 447-469.
- Barnes, S. B. (2006). A privacy paradox: Social networking in the United States. First Monday, 11(9).
- Walther, J. B., Van Der Heide, B., Kim, S. Y., Westerman, D., & Tong, S. T. (2008). The role of friends' appearance and behavior on evaluations of individuals on Facebook: Are we known by the company we keep?. Human Communication Research, 34(1), 28-49.
- Stutzman, F. (2006). An evaluation of identity-sharing behavior in social network communities. International Digital and Media Arts Journal, 3(1), 10-18.

CHAPTER VIII

Social Networking and its addictions

- Karaiskos, D., Tzavellas, E., Balta, G., & Paparrigopoulos, T. (2010). P02-232-Social network addiction: a new clinical disorder? European Psychiatry, 25, 855.

- Song, I., Larose, R., Eastin, M. S., & Lin, C. A. (2004). Internet gratifications and Internet addiction: On the uses and abuses of new media. CyberPsychology & Behavior, 7(4), 384-394.
- Young, K. S. (1998). Internet addiction: The emergence of a new clinical disorder. CyberPsychology & Behavior, 1(3), 237-244.
- Young, K. S. (1999). Internet addiction: symptoms, evaluation and treatment. Innovations in clinical practice: A source book, 17, 19-31.
- Young, K. S. (2004). Internet addiction a new clinical phenomenon and its consequences. American behavioral scientist, 48(4), 402-415.

CHAPTER IX
Social Media ethics

- Bassett, E. H., & O'Riordan, K. (2002). Ethics of Internet research: Contesting the human subjects research model. Ethics and Information Technology, 4(3), 233-247.
- Birky, I., & Collins, W. (2011). Facebook: Maintaining ethical practice in the cyberspace age. Journal of College Student Psychotherapy, 25(3), 193-203.
- Bruckman, A., Karahalios, K., Kraut, R. E., Poole, E. S., Thomas, J. C., & Yardi, S. (2010). Revisiting research ethics in the Facebook era: challenges in emerging CSCW research. In The 2010 Conference on Computer Supported Cooperative Work, Savannah, Georgia.

✦ Hudson, J. M., & Bruckman, A. (2005, January). Using empirical data to reason about internet research ethics. In ECSCW 2005 (pp. 287-306). Springer Netherlands.

✦ Light, B., & McGrath, K. (2010). Ethics and social networking sites: a disclosive analysis of Facebook. Information Technology & People, 23(4), 290-311.

✦ Light, B., Mcgrath, K., & Griffiths, M. (2008). Facebook's ethics. Facebook: A Network, A Research Tool, A World.

✦ Light, B., McGrath, K., & Griffiths, M. (2008). More than just friends? Facebook, disclosive ethics and the morality of technology. ICIS 2008 proceedings, 193.

✦ Zimmer, M. (2010). "But the data is already public": on the ethics of research in Facebook. Ethics and information technology, 12(4), 313-325.

CHAPTER X

Role of social media in nation building

✦ Charnigo, L., & Barnett-Ellis, P. (2013). Checking out Facebook. com: the impact of a digital trend on academic libraries. Information technology and libraries, 26(1), 23-34.

✦ Gajjala, R. (2007). Shifting frames: Race, ethnicity, and intercultural communication in online social networking and virtual work. The role of communication in business transactions and relationships, 257-276.

✦ Hansen, D., Shneiderman, B., & Smith, M. A. (2010). Analyzing social media networks with NodeXL: Insights from a connected world. Morgan Kaufmann.

- Kaplan, A. M., & Haenlein, M. (2010). Users of the world, unite! The challenges and opportunities of social media. Business horizons, 53(1), 59-68.
- Kaplan, A. M., & Haenlein, M. (2012). Social media: back to the roots and back to the future. Journal of Systems and Information Technology, 14(2), 101-104.
- Mahajan, P. (2009). Use of social networking in a linguistically and culturally rich India. The International Information & Library Review, 41(3), 129-136.
- Perkel, D. (2010). Copy and paste literacy? Literacy practices in the production of a MySpace profile. Trabalhos em Linguística Aplicada, 49(2), 493-511.
- Postill, J. (2008). Media and nation building: How the Iban became Malaysian (Vol. 1). Berghahn Books.

CHAPTER XI

Status of political parties in social media

- Cogburn, D. L., & Espinoza-Vasquez, F. K. (2011). From networked nominee to networked nation: Examining the impact of Web 2.0 and social media on political participation and civic engagement in the 2008 Obama campaign. Journal of Political Marketing, 10(1-2), 189-213.

WEB RESOURCES

- https://www.facebook.com/BJP4India?fref=ts
- https://www.facebook.com/narendramodi?fref=ts

https://www.facebook.com/AamAadmiParty?fref=ts

- https://www.facebook.com/AAPkaArvind?fref=ts https://www.facebook.com IndianNationalCongress?fref=ts
- https://twitter.com/AamAadmiParty
- https://twitter.com/BJP4India
- https://twitter.com/narendramodi
- www.bjp.org
- www.inc.in
- www.aamaadmiparty.org
- http://www.socialsamosa.com/electiontracker/.

APPENDIX 1

Interview Transcript

Interview of main three Political parties, Social Media Heads: (Vishesh Singh, Social Media Head, All India Congress Committee) – Interviewed by- Dr. Sanjay Singh Baghel and Ashish Dwevedi.

Q. What was your campaign strategy on SM?

Ans.: Strictly talking about our own campaign, our only fault was that we arrived late on the scene. As far as other factors of SM campaigning are concerned, I think it was a well-balanced campaign with a positive note. Since we were late, our strategy tended to be reactive rather than proactive as far as Lok Sabha election-2014 is concerned. Later we engaged proactively on some level, for example we decided to take public sentiments into account when drafting our election manifesto, both on online as well as offline forums.

Q. Sir, as compared to AAP or BJP your campaign lacked visibility? What went wrong in that regard?

Ans.: See, social media works like a chain reaction, so even if anyone is slightly ahead of you, he has got a definite lead. We arrived late and paid the price for it, even a smaller party like AAP went ahead of us. As far as AAP is concerned, it originated through social media and what BJP did right was that they started way earlier. It's not like they ran a perfect campaign, but they started earlier. One of the shortcomings that I see in BJP's SM campaign was that for the early 2-3 years their campaign had entirely negative connotation. They took on prominent Congress leader's individually and ran a vicious, negative campaign against them, discrediting them. One case in point being, Digvijaya Singh for whom very coarse language was used. Rahul Gandhi and Kapil Sibel were other prominent targets in this negative campaign. BJP stuck to the theory that if a lie is repeated 100 times it becomes the truth. They exploited the gullibility of today's youth for whom SM has become the prominent source of information. The propaganda by BJP was unmatched; A Chinese road's picture was shown as Ahmadabad's BRT. There are many such instances. Mr. Modi was projected as the savior of the people, larger than life, and by the time we arrived, the lies were established, damage had been done. Mainstream media fully co-operated with BJP in its propaganda mission. News networks owned by pro-BJP industrialists sang their tune 24X7. We failed in traditional media-management and BJP's strong hold on SM proved detrimental for our electoral prospects.

Q. Which platforms and tools you used for SM campaigning?

Ans.: We utilized online sentiment measuring to check the effectiveness of the tags we used in our SM campaign. We also tracked the frequency with which tags of the opposition as well as our won were used on SM, both positively and negatively. When it comes to platforms, we used Facebook, Twitter, YouTube and since we are in reactive mode, wherever our opposition was we had to be there.

Q. What is the percentage of your leaders who were active on SM?

Ans.: Defining a percentage is a difficult task because for that one has to define 100 prominent leaders of the party and then determine the percentage. Roughly speaking, it should be around 25-40%. Kapil Sibel, Digvijaya Singh, Jyotiraditya Scindia used it extensively and very effectively. Other leaders were present but did not use it. PM had his official handle but used it rarely. Rahul Gandhi and Sonia ji were absent entirely. The conspicuous absence of the captain and vice-captain somewhat diminished the effectiveness of our campaign.

Q. How did the absence of your two prominent leaders, Mr. Rahul Gandhi, and Sonia Ji, with whom Congress party is still identified with, affect your campaign?

Ans.: A lot of negative propaganda was around for these two people and since they were not present, they could not even counter these falsehoods. It was entirely their own decision and a personal choice. They are very young but shy about it and there are people very old but used it effectively. Dipendar Singh Hudda is one such leader and his father too became active in SM.

Yes, the absence of captain and vice-captain did affect the impression of people, but I would not say performance. The falsehoods propagated by other parties gained foothold because they were not there to explain it.

Q. Sir, Modi ji, projects himself as a media-savvy, especially SM, leader but the same cannot be said about the leadership of Congress. Why is that?

Ans.: See, it's more about image-building. Modi Ji's image appears on social media holding a map while taking an aerial survey of cyclone-affected areas and he is eulogized incessantly but when Mr. or Ms. Gandhi does the same, they are portrayed as if they were picnicking. What we lacked here is a good performance in marketing. But you can fool some people for some time but you cannot fool all the people all the time. This media-created bubble will burst. People will buy the bad product for once due to this blitzkrieg of marketing but eventually they will return to the good one. Without a shadow of doubt BJP is way better in marketing than us. They did it during the elections and are doing it when they are in power. Taking credits for the schemes that we conceived.

Modi ji appears on National news channel, and he rarely takes questions. There is originating a culture of one-way interaction where half-truths are presented as gospel truth. Even if there is a slight voice of reason and sanity it is drowned by the sheer cacophony of sounds that is surrounding Modi ji. Things will unfold in 4th year when people ask for the report card.

Q. Sir, what is the expenditure incurred by Congress in your SM campaign?

Ans.: I cannot divulge specific amount we spent but I can assure you that BJP's expenditure was 20 times more than us. That showed visibility which was 10 times better than us.

Q. How are you channelizing your SM campaign in terms of youth outreach?

Ans.: We have a dedicated SM team headed by Dipender Singh Hudda Ji and this team manages SM campaign of INC. In terms of content, we stick to the facts. BJP usually works through surrogates and runs a negative campaign. Subrahmanyam Swami, Baba Ramdev being case in point. The top leadership of BJP normally talks positively on SM but there is an active brigade at the down level tasked with mud-slinging and other dirty tactics.

Q. Sir, you talked about presence and visibility but when it comes to engagement level you stood far behind BJP and even AAP.

Ans.: See, few people like what is healthy, most go towards spicy. That is what happened here, we presented cold-hard truths and they lie in beautiful wraps. Naturally, people went towards it.

Q. Sir since the strategy you depended on so far faired rather badly. So, what would be the future strategy of INC?

Ans.: As incumbent that was only strategy available to us. However, as opposition perhaps we can try out some more strategies, more proactive in nature. Ultimately, the better product would be recognized.

Q. So can we assume that you are going to adopt this kind of strategy in upcoming Delhi elections?

Ans.: IN Delhi we are in opposition, so we are going to be proactive this time and highlight the shortcomings of the government. The schemes that were launched by INC are stalled now.

Q. Sir, you were leading on SM in Haryana, but results came out different. How do we perceive this change?

Ans.: In Haryana SM still plays a very small part, compared to urban population. Combined with the 10 years of anti-incumbency it affected our overall performance.

Q. But Sir anti-incumbency factor was there in Gujarat, Madhya Pradesh, and Chhattisgarh too.

Ans.: I would say it depends on two major factors, how you handle opposition and media. Sheila Ji served for 3 consecutive terms too. Our opposition highlighted our mistakes very effectively and we failed to highlight our successful policies and growth momentum.

Q. So what would be your strategy in future when it comes to countering a personality-centric campaign with a leader who enjoys mass appeal?

Ans.: See, admittedly we have few leaders in Congress who enjoy the kind of mass support Modi ji seems to have right now, not even close. Very few senior leaders have passed the electoral test and there seem to be a lack of challengers for Modi ji. And who do have mass-support, their reluctance to come on SM is one of the causes behind Modi Ji's grand success. On SM, whoever engages is popular, doesn't matter if he is writing negatively or positively. The lack of defence from prominent INC leaders adds to the growing perception that they are reluctant.

(Navrang, Social Media Head, BJP)- Interviewed by- Dr. Sanjay Singh Baghel and Ashish Dwevedi.

Q. Sir, How SM has changed the political campaigning?

Ans.: Well. Earlier the communication was one way, controlled. You can't tell a news paper editor to write what you want but SM is an open forum. We can write what we want. This helped us to reach out to a wider audience educating them about our policies and our manifesto. Through SM, the communication gap was bridged.

Q. Sir, what makes your strategy so successful, vis-à-vis INC and AAP?

Ans.: In context of general elections, as a leader we had Narendra Modi Ji who already had a proven track record of governance, be it industrial, education or social welfare. So, there was a hope that this man can do something if given a chance. Our work on SM was to make people aware of that. We started our FB page in 2010 to communicate with people effectively. When we lost General Elections in 2009, we realized that the SM, as an open forum would play a larger role in 2014 and we got to create our strategy according to it. This early decision put us in a very favourable position, and we gained the first-mover advantage. We recognized the scale and importance of SM way before anyone did and that helped us immensely. We had a great product which could be marketed with minimum efforts. Since 2012, we gradually made our points what we will do if voted in power, Sri Narendra Modi ji as the leader. We created our manifesto and released a charge sheet against INC highlighting the shortcomings of the government and pointing how would we tackle them if voted in power. And as you can see, we are gradually following the promises made in our manifesto.

Q. What was your target audience on SM?

Ans.: 18-24.

Q. Congress and AAP often say that BJP has excellent marketing strategy for an inferior product, and you say you have the best product which is supported by an effective marketing strategy. Who is nearer the truth?

Ans.: This question has been answered by the people of India very effectively and I don't think it's time to go into that debate.

Q. Other than Facebook and twitter which other platforms and tools you used in your SM campaign?

Ans.: We adopted a very inclusive and through campaign strategy. We gave equal importance to FB, Twitter, WhatsApp, SMS campaigning. We always design a 360-degree campaign. The same contents we used across the platforms.

Q. was there any dedicated team for this purpose or you took services of an advertising agency?

Ans.: We had a creative team here, volunteers chosen from different backgrounds. We had a team of 40 who engaged in brainstorming on what kind of messages should be broadcast, the theme of campaign, content, design.

Q. How much BJP spend during the LS elections on SM campaign?

Ans. We are at not liberty to divulge that kind of information. SM is driven by people anyway; you cannot drive it with money. Most of our campaign management was undertaken by volunteers. We had volunteers from Singapore, US, Mumbai etc. Campaign obviously costs but it was driven by people. There was a rumour that we hired many IT-cells to disseminate our SM campaign. That was completely baseless, and I have to say this kind of confusion that our opposition had ultimately proved harmful for them.

Q. Sir, your engagement level was excellent all throughout the campaign. Was it entirely content driven?

Ans.: See, SM is not only about Twitter, Facebook, and all. It's about personal engagement. For example, we had a volunteer who would mark the twitter handle tweeting positive tweets about BJP and compile a list of many such handles. In this way we created a support base, we messaged them personally and engaged with them on a personal level. We launched several 78200-78200 for volunteers. We engaged with them via WhatsApp and email too.

Q. How did you channelize this?

Ans.: We organized Volunteers meet-ups. In fact, first such meet was held way back in 2011, just to evaluate our presence on SM. We invited 200 people from SM and more than 150 showed up at our Delhi-office. They were not members of BJP or office bearers or had anything to do with BJP before that. In 2012, we organized such meets on a bigger scale in 7-8 big cities across India including Bangalore, Lucknow, Mumbai etc. IN 2013, when we had a cleared view of elections, we upped the ante and organized such meets even in the small towns too. We engaged people. It's not like we trended some tags on Twitter and win elections, those who did now see the results. Elections eventually are about mandate not about Facebook or twitter. Our strategy was to convert our online presence into votes on ground, and that we did spectacularly well. We had a small team dedicated towards integration of online and offline campaign.

Q. As a medium of reach, what percentage do you think SM contributed?

Ans.: At least in 160 constituencies the influence of SM was critical. We categorized seats according to the reach of this medium and devised our strategy, accordingly, based on our own internal analysis. At some places it was 20% or 30% and we focused our energy towards utilizing it effectively. Our young energetic volunteers maximized the influence of SM campaign combined with local BJP workers' work. This group formed the backbone of our campaign.

Q.: What kind of facilities did you provide, if any, for this seamless integration of offline and online campaign?

Ans.: Yes, we provided them campaign materials but no, we did not provide them any expenses since they were all volunteers.

Q.: How was your Lok Sabha election campaign different from state elections? Considering the factors such as language barrier, low internet reach, local issues among other things.

Ans.: at state elections our campaign was more simple and rather easy. We created videos, songs in local languages and distributed them widely. As in Jharkhand where among tribals such as Santhals we used their folk songs when creating campaign material. Haryana was easy because of the homogeneity of the language.

Q.: During the LS elections, BJP used 3D projections of Modi Ji's rallies extensively. What was the role of SM in that?

Ans.: We requested our volunteers to play those in their local areas, through laptops and projectors. As in Sonipat, our volunteers would set up projector and screen on the days of a rally and would broadcast it to the local audience live.

Q.: According to an article on Daily Mail, you had 40-member team dedicated to SM campaign. Were they all professionals on a part time basis or is it your permanent strength?

Ans.: That's not our permanent strength. Most of them were volunteers who contributed during LS. People from varied backgrounds were part of it.

Q.: So what is the current strength of your IT-cell? Are they paid by party or volunteers?

Ans.: Right now, we have 10 members and as far as I know that most of them are volunteers.

Q.: Are there State IT-cells of BJP?

Ans.: Yes, we have state IT-cells, district IT-cells and we are also establishing IT-cells at commissions as well. SM campaign cannot be driven by money, in fact no campaign can be successful only by money unless there is a wide public engagement involved. We don't need agencies because we have strength of people. Since the launch of membership drive, we have already registered more than 3 crore people within two months. We engaged with people and used this strength to our advantage in campaigning and in donation drives.

Q.: According to a news article, in your successful SM campaign, NRI push played a key role. What kind of role they played and to what extent?

Ans.: We had 8-10 people here from abroad who took a job break just to participate in our campaign. Around 20-15% of our volunteers were NRIs. There was a lady who was in-charge of women IT-cell.

Q.: What is next, since now you are in government and your task is now to defend rather than accuse?

Ans.: The government and party are totally separate entities. We as a party have nothing to do with the government. Government has its own apparatus to defend itself. Every ministry has its own twitter handle, Modi Ji has made sure the transparency in governance. Our responsibility is to increase our presence in states where we lack visibility such as Orissa, Kerala, Tamandu etc. to include new members. Our plate is already full.

Q.: There is a general allegation that all three parties have used SM more as negative propaganda tool than positive informational medium. For example, AAP accused BJP of manipulating contents and spreading misinformation through SM citing the Ahmedabad BRT's photo which was of China's.

Ans.: SM is an open forum and there are disadvantages of it. If a individual entry is posting something that should not be taken as an endorsement by the party and it should not reflect badly on the party itself. And as far as manipulation of content through SM in context of political campaigning is concerned, BJP is staunchly against that. It's wrong.

Q.: But this allegation is there that SM has been used to mislead people. How do you counter that?

Ans.: You can find the answer to this question just by having a cursory glance at our over all campaign. Visit our Facebook page and look at the content. You will find only positive material there. We did not use SM or any tool for manipulations or spreading lies or misleading people. Similarly, you can have a look at our Tweets during the LS campaign too. We relied on fair criticism and highlighting our own achievements in BJP ruled states.

Q.: Who is the head of IT-Cell of BJP?

Ans.: Arvind Gupta is the head of IT-Cell and Mr. Navrang heads the SM unit of IT-cell. Apart from that, we have a dedicated team.

(Ankit Lal, Head Social media and IT cell, AAP)- Interviewed by- Ashish Dwevedi.

Q.: How social media has changed the face of political campaigning in India?

Ans.: Before social media arrived on the scene, leaders were more or less clueless about what people were talking about. There was a huge disconnect with the people, the constituents. SM has to certain extents, bridged that communication gap. The people on SM talk about things express their views. Although it is not 100% reliable, it gives certain ideas of the things that people are mostly relating to and are talking about.

Q.: One practice that has been very prevalent on social media campaigning is artificially created 'Likes', 'followers' etc. as with the paid news problem in conventional media, this practice obscures the clear picture. So, does SM still present the reflection of the people who are potential voters?

Ans.: Well, you can buy number of followers and likes but cannot buy engagement. Even a cursory glance at the engagement levels and stats of three main political parties including AAP shows that despite a fraction of the budget dedicated to SM campaigning as compared to other two parties, the engagement levels of AAP are very high. When you take the engagement part, especially the organic engagement part, though Facebook has reduced the number of organic views drastically over one year, but still organic views constitute a large number of views that all the parties get especially now a days because we tried to create organic content which is attractive in some manner so for us the engagement levels are high.

Q.: Recently, the outsourcing of SM campaign of a prominent political leader was in the news. Is this practice, of outsourcing the campaign, more effective?

Ans.: A corporate house cannot understand a political ideology, profit being the sole motive. Whatever it takes it is very difficult for a person sitting in a corporate house to understand what decisions you are making and for what results. There is always this call-to-action that we have. We do something and expect the audience to react to that in a certain manner. However, with paid campaigning it is very difficult for political parties to grasp what is going on, defeating the entire purpose of a SM campaigning.

Q.: Sir about the political ideologies, you mentioned in an ET interview that you were influenced by JP movement. In this age of 140-character activism has SM robbed the ideologies of its essence, distorting them beyond comprehension turning them mere rhetoric or has it constructively contributed to the spread of ideologies and their interpretations?

Ans.: See, you can't deliver ideology in 140 characters but even a book is too small to effectively deliver an ideology so ideology can't be delivered in a very short period, it has to be through sustained efforts. It took us nearly two years to get through our ideology of Swaraj to people, to make even 1 percent of people understand what Swaraj actually means and even then, only a fraction of them were able to grasp the essence of the ideology. So, until and unless we implement it and give it a practical example to the people, it is very difficult for people to ascertain what exactly the ideology stands for. One good example of this is the currently much talked about 'Hindutva' ideology. Even the staunchest supporters of the ideology seem to have different approaches towards it.

Q.: Has SM been used more as negative propaganda machine than an informational tool?

Ans.: Different categories of people have used it in different manner. Some people have used it to propagate very good things. In India, we have utilized the power of social media in a very effective manner but at the same time it has been misused very badly especially the rapid mobilization power of SM. The audience will grow, will mature as the time passes so instead incidents such as hate-mongering through WhatsApp messages that played a pivotal role in Muzaffarnagar riots will decrease and noble initiatives like Ice Bucket challenge will find better, matured audience.

However, there is a stark difference between negative campaigning and honest questioning, the right to dissent, latter being cornerstone of a democracy.

Q.: but so far as we have seen it has been mostly used in negative propaganda. Few people have grasped the idea of

Swaraj but millions became agitated over a fake circulating video?

Ans.: Every innovative breakthrough in human history has been first used for nefarious purposes and then for the greater good. Be it nuclear technology, missile technology or even the internet. The same has happened with SM. SM will grow and mature over next ten years.

Q.: With the new style of governance that we are seeing, where emphasis is on direct communication with the people through social media, would this trend lead to marginalization of conventional media? Are there any clashes between the SM and conventional media?

Ans.: In India, the people on SM is a fraction of the total population, somewhere between 10-15%. What about the rest of the 90% for whom the source of information is still the conventional media. In the current scenario, conventional media cannot be marginalized. However, the gist of news, the USP of news has shifted to SM because of its speed, nothing else. Mainstream media is still the force and will remain so at least for the next 5-10 years. The news-breaking capacity of conventional media has shifted to the social media, but the propagation mechanism is still more or less the same. Social media is as of now limited to breaking news.

Q.: Sir, as we have seen over few years that the SM has radically changed the way information is consumed and distributed. Does it also have any impact whatsoever on how the information is perceived as opposed to conventional information tools?

Ans.: Yes definitely, that has changed. The perception has changed a lot just because the way information is portrayed has evolved.

Q.: Sir in context of political campaigning, as we have seen that AAP always had the upper hand quite drastically over Congress and was just marginally behind BJP but when it came to the actual vote share, the trends on SM proved to be misleading. What went wrong?

Ans.: As I have already said, SM is but a minor percentage of what India really is, in next 5-10 years that situation will definitely change but right now we are just two-year-old party. The very fact that we were able to match them on ideological level in the national elections shows that we have the ability and potential. But our organization, our grass-root level reach there is a lot that we want from ourselves and eventually it will happen. AAP is an idea that will take time to sprout and flourish but it is something that is bound to happen.

Q.: Sir, what is the underlining social media strategy of AAP?

Ans.: Engagement matters. Just keep engaging with people. Interaction is the key, not propagation. We listen to people and respond. We have created a two-way channel for interaction.

Q.: Has AAP's SM strategy changed or even slightly altered after general elections?

Ans.: After General elections, all of us eased a bit because we had been in a regular campaigning mode for last one and a half year approximately. We took time off to cater to our personal commitments. In AAP's SM team there are four members who work full time and around 200 working on part-time basis. Due to the personal commitments, there was a marginal slump after the general elections but now things are back on track, and everything is looking good again.

Q.: What is the SM strategy for upcoming assembly elections in Maharashtra and Haryana?

Ans.: IN both states, we are not fighting as of now but still we are trying to engage with people, educate them and help them choose a right candidate.

Q.: Sir, is it safe to say that AAP has moved back towards online activism rather than active political campaigning?

Ans.: We were always activists. We were activists who were pushed into politics because the main political parties were not ready to accept the genuine and long overdue demand of anti-corruption bill. It is that simple, we are not politicians at all.

Q.: Sir, during the recent protests against UPSC, the social media particularly twitter was conspicuously almost silent (relatively speaking), do you think the language bias here also played a crucial role?

Ans.: No, because if you see at least AAP took a stand about it. We did press conferences and on twitter many of us were active and especially were trying to quash the rumors regarding the CSAT circulating on SM. Our strategy was not to fuel that divide but to quite the rumors that were going around.

Q.: Among the two main political parties who do you find closer to your practices, ethics, and strategies in terms of social media campaigning?

Ans.: Actually no one does. Congress' SM strategy seems to be the glorification of few people by any means necessary and BJP is more about track. So, we don't actually find any of them any closer to ours.

Q.: AAP had already a base due to IAC movement on SM before party's actual debut on social media. What were the initial challenges in online activism and then moving towards political campaigning?

Ans.: The biggest and foremost challenge was to convince the people that we have founded a party and to explain them the reason why we did so.

Q.: What is the biggest crisis you have faced during the campaigning, SM or otherwise?

Ans.: There has been situations but we don't consider them crisis situations. We regard them as lean periods and spurts. On certain occasions there were candidates who were attacked that time we had to take it to the people very seriously. But generally, we don't have crisis situations as such.

Q.: In terms of SM campaign and outreach, what are the factors that separate AAP from other parties?

Ans.: Our focus is on positive campaigning not propaganda. We take facts, present to people, and let them decide what is right or what is wrong. We don't tell them that this is good for you, and this is not. We just present the situation as it is. Also, our focus is on clean campaigning where transparency is of utmost importance. Every paisa we spend in the campaigning is accounted for. How many parties can say such thing? Our volunteer culture, the backbone of our SM campaign is unparalleled.

Q.: Sir, do you think that with social issues like 'Nirbhaya case' social media is more charitable than towards political causes like corruption or electoral reforms?

Ans.: It is basically human nature. This kind of contents touches the common sentiments sooner than political issues which take time for a deep impact. To certain extents, the much less enthusiasm for political causes can be attributed to the cynicism which has crept into the mindset of the masses regarding the issues political in nature. All of us like to show other people that we are good humans this is why social causes find better and far more eager audience than political ones. In essence, it is about psychology and not much to do with SM as such.

Q.: Sir, last question. How can SM contribute to nation building?

Ans.: There is various ways in which SM can contribute. There have been certain examples when it has, it can be used during crisis situations, for political awareness and for social causes which is already being heavily used. It can also be used for engaging wit people in your own area specially to tackle corruption. There are horizons that are waiting to be opened through SM. The possibilities are endless.

Thank You.

Appendix 2

Questionnaire on Social Networking Sites

Social Networking Sites (SNS) is a recent emergence that has brought a complete revolution. There is a great deal of speculation about its influence on the user's lives. The study intends to examine the awareness, usage and purposes of SNS and its likely impact on the life styles of Indian Youth. The questionnaire is part of our research project on the topic ''Impact of SNS on the Indian youth: A study of their life styles and its effectiveness in nation building" and has been framed to seek your feedback and opinion on the same. The questionnaire is strictly confidential and its results would be used only for research purpose keeping the anonymity of the respondent and his/her responses. Therefore, please give true and fair responses. The questionnaire has three sections. Please attempt all.

*** Required**

Top of Form

SECTION I
PERSONAL INFORMATION

Name (optional) ☐

Gender

☐ Male

☐ Female

Age

☐ Below 20 years

☐ 20 – 30 years

☐ 30 – 40 years

☐ Above 40 years

Educational Qualifications

☐ Graduation

☐ Post Graduation

Other: Category

☐ Student

☐ Working

☐ Not Working

Income

☐ None

☐ 10000 – 30000

☐ 30000 – 50000

☐ Above 50000

SECTION II

TYPES OF SOCIAL NETWORKING SITES AND THEIR USAGE

A. Do you currently have an account on any Social Networking Site (SNS)?

- ◯ Yes
- ◯ No

B. If no, why not? (Tick the right answer)

- ◯ Do not have regular computer access.
- ◯ Do not have time
- ◯ Not interested
- ◯ Not aware of any Social Network site
- ◯ None of the above

If you answered 'Yes" to question A, please continue further.

1. Which SNS are you are a member?

- ◯ Flicker
- ◯ Facebook
- ◯ Twitter
- ◯ Orkut
- ◯ LinkedIn
- ◯ My space
- ◯ Hi5
- ◯ WhatsApp

Other: [ ]

2. **Since how long have you been a member of the SNS?**

☐

3. **How many hours in a week do you spend on these SNS?**

- ○ 0 – 5 hours
- ○ 6 – 10 hours
- ○ 11 - 20 hours
- ○ 21- 30 hours
- ○ 31 – 40 hours
- ○ More than 40 hours

4. **What information about yourself do you include in your SNS? (You may select more than one)**

- ☐ Name / identity
- ☐ Email
- ☐ Hometown/ city
- ☐ Instant messenger address
- ☐ Mobile number
- ☐ Photos
- ☐ Relationship status
- ☐ Date of birth
- ☐ Place of work
- ☐ Interests/ likes
- ☐ Other:

5. **Indicate the purpose(s) for which you use the SNS**

- [ ] Chatting & messaging
- [ ] Networking & developing contacts.
- [ ] Sharing & uploading pictures
- [ ] Checking status of others
- [ ] Updating your status
- [ ] Seeking & giving information
- [ ] Entertainment
- [ ] Education & knowledge
- [ ] Job opportunities & employment
- [ ] Online shopping
- [ ] Expressing opinions on different issues
- [ ] Other:

SECTION III

Impact and Influence of SNS

(Please tick your choice)

1. **Being part of these Social Networking Sites is important and significant in today's scenario.**

Strongly Agree	Agree	Disagree	Strongly Disagree
○	○	○	○

2. **For me my profile and updates reflect my status and personality**

Strongly Agree	Agree	Disagree	Strongly Disagree
○	○	○	○

3. **I feel that the privacy of my Personal information is protected on these sites.**

Strongly Agree	Agree	Disagree	Strongly Disagree
○	○	○	○

4. **I trust that these Social Networking Sites will not use my personal information for any other purpose**

Strongly Agree	Agree	Disagree	Strongly Disagree
○	○	○	○

5. **I believe that the information which I collect through these sites is absolutely correct.**

Strongly Agree	Agree	Disagree	Strongly Disagree
○	○	○	○

6. **Social Networking Sites have an important influence on my lifestyle with respect to ***

¬ Personal growth and development

Strongly Agree	Agree	Disagree	Strongly Disagree
○	○	○	○

¬ Professional growth

Strongly Agree	Agree	Disagree	Strongly Disagree
○	○	○	○

¬ Relationships

Strongly Agree	Agree	Disagree	Strongly Disagree
○	○	○	○

¬ Education and knowledge

Strongly Agree	Agree	Disagree	Strongly Disagree
○	○	○	○

¬ Health and Fitness

Strongly Agree	Agree	Disagree	Strongly Disagree
○	○	○	○

7. **SNS are relevant and effective platforms to discuss Socio-economic issues (like human rights, women harassment, sexual assaults, gender discrimination, environment concerns etc.)**

Strongly Agree	Agree	Disagree	Strongly Disagree
○	○	○	○

8. **In the recent past political concerns and issues in our country has gained momentum through social networking and it had a major impact on recent Lok Sabha Election?**

Strongly Agree	Agree	Disagree	Strongly Disagree
○	○	○	○

9. **Do you believe that in recent Lok Sabha elections Modi and Kejriwal gained a new brand identity due to social media?**

Strongly Agree	Agree	Disagree	Strongly Disagree
○	○	○	○

10. Believe groups/ communities on these sites that are involved in social/ political issues or are working to advance such causes to bring about awareness in public.

Strongly Agree	Agree	Disagree	Strongly Disagree
○	○	○	○

11. I feel in the near future social media can play a significant role for national development.

Strongly Agree	Agree	Disagree	Strongly Disagree
○	○	○	○